a million little pieces

I know.

The sooner the better, but if you want we can wait.

The sooner the better.

All right.

He spreads his feet and he firms himself and he puts both of his hands on my nose. I grab the sides of the bed and I close my eyes and I wait.

You ready?

Yeah.

He jerks his hands forward and up and there's an audible crack. Cold white light shoots through my eyes and through my spine and into my feet and back again. My eyes are closed but I'm crying. Blood is streaming from my nostrils.

Now I have to set it.

He moves his hands to the side and I can feel the cartilage move with them. He moves them again. I can feel it. He presses up and it seems to fit. I can feel it.

There.

He reaches for some tape and I open my eyes. He puts the tape across the bridge of my nose and it holds the cartilage in place. It feels solid.

He grabs a towel and he wipes the blood from my face and my neck and I stare at the wall. My face is throbbing and I'm squeezing the sides of the bed and it hurts my hands. I want to let go but I can't.

You all right?

No.

I can't give you any painkillers.

I figured.

The Librium and Diazepam will take the edge off, but you're gonna hurt.

I know.

I'll get you a new robe.

Thank you.

He steps back and he throws the towel in the garbage can and he leaves. I let go of the bed and I hold my hands in front of my face and I stare at them. They shake, I shake.

The Doctor comes back with a Nurse and they help me change and they tell me about the tests they're going to give me. Blood, urine, stool. They need to know how much damage I've done to my insides. The thought revolts me.

We leave and we go to a different Room that also has a Bathroom. I piss in a cup, shit in a plastic container, take a needle in my arm. It's simple and it's easy and it's painless.

We emerge and the Unit is busy. Patients wait in line for drugs, Doctors go from Room to Room, Nurses carry bottles and tubes. There is noise, but everything is quiet.

I go to my Room with the Doctor and I sit on the bed. He sits in the chair and he
writes on a chart. He finishes writing and he looks at me.
Except for the Dentist, the worst of it is over.
All right.
I'm going to put you on two hundred and fifty milligrams of Amoxicillin three
times a day and five hundred milligrams of Penicillin VK once a day. These
will prevent any possible infection.
All right.
Go to the Dispensary and they'll give them to you, or if you forget, a Nurse
will come find you.
Okay.
Thank you for dealing this morning.
No problem.
Good luck.
Thanks.
He stands and I stand and we shake hands and he leaves. I go to the
Dispensary and I stand in line. A young woman stands in front of me. She
turns around and she looks at my face. She speaks.
Hi.
She smiles.
Hi.
She holds out her hand.
I'm Lilly.
I take it. It's soft and warm.
I'm James.
I don't want to let go, but I do. We step forward.
What happened?
She glances toward the Dispensary.
I don't remember.
She turns back.
Blacked out?
Yeah.
She grimaces.
Shit.
I laugh.
Yeah.
We step forward.
When'd you get here?
I glance toward the Dispensary.
Yesterday.
The Nurse is glaring.
Me too.
I motion toward the Nurse and Lilly turns around and she stops talking and

we step forward and we wait. The Nurse glares at us and she hands Lilly some pills and a cup of water and Lilly takes the pills and she drinks the water. She turns around and as she passes me she smiles and she mouths the word bye. I smile and step forward. The Nurse glares at me and asks me my name.

James Frey.

She looks at a chart and she goes to a cabinet and she gets some pills and she hands them to me with a cup of water.

I take the pills.

I drink the water.

I go to my Room and I fall asleep and I spend the rest of the day sleeping and shoving food down my throat and waiting in line and taking pills.

It's still dark when my body wakes me. My insides burn and feel like fire. They move and the pain comes. They move again and the pain becomes greater. They move again and I am paralyzed.

I know what's coming and I need to get up but I can't walk, so I roll off the bed and I fall to the floor. I lie there and I moan and it's cold and silent and dark.

The pain subsides and I crawl into the Bathroom and I grab the sides of the toilet and I wait. I sweat and my breath is short and my heart palpitates. My body lurches and I close my eyes and I lean forward. Blood and bile and chunks of my stomach come pouring from my mouth and my nose. It gets stuck in my throat, in my nostrils, in what remains of my teeth. Again it comes, again it comes, again it comes, and with each episode a sharp pain shoots through my chest, my left arm and my jaw. I bang my head on the back of the toilet but I feel nothing. I bang it again. Nothing.

The vomiting stops and I sit back and I open my eyes and I stare at the toilet. Thick red streams stick to its sides and brown pieces of my interior float in the water. I try to slow my breathing and my heart but I can't, so I sit and I wait. Every morning it's the same. I vomit and I sit and I wait.

After a few minutes I stand and I walk slowly back into the Room. Night is leaving and I stand at the window and I watch. Orange and pink streaks sail across the blue of the sky, large birds silhouette themselves against the red of the rising sun, clouds inch their way toward me. I can feel blood dripping from the wounds on my face and I can feel my heart beating and I can feel the weight of my life beginning to drop and I realize why dawn is called mourning.

I wipe my face with my sleeve and I take off my robe, which is now covered with blood and whatever I just threw up and I drop it on the floor and I go to the Bathroom. I turn on the shower and I wait for the warm water.

I look at my body. My skin is sallow and white. My torso is covered with cuts and bruises. I'm thin and my muscles sag. I look worn, beaten, old, dead. I didn't always look like this.

I reach in and I feel the water. It's warm, but not hot. I step inside the shower and I turn off the cold water and I wait for the heat.

The water runs down my chest and along the rest of my body. I take a bar of soap and I lather up and as I do, the water becomes hotter. It slams into my skin and burns my skin and turns my skin red. Although it hurts, it feels good. The heat, the water, the soap, the burns. It hurts but I deserve it.

I turn off the water and I step out of the shower and I dry myself off. I climb into bed and I climb under the covers and I close my eyes and I try to remember. Eight days ago I was in North Carolina. I remember picking up a bottle and a pipe and deciding to go for a drive. Two days later I woke up in Washington, D.C. I was on a couch at a House belonging to the Sister of a friend of mine. I was covered in piss and puke and she wanted me to leave so I borrowed a shirt from her and I left. Twenty-four hours later I woke up in Ohio. I remember a House, a Bar, some crack, some glue. I remember screaming. I remember crying.

The door opens and I sit up and the Doctor brings in a pile of clothes and my pills and he sets them on the table.

Hi.

I reach for the pills.

Hi.

I take them.

We got you some fresh clothes.

Thanks.

He sits at the table.

We're going to move you down to a Unit today.

All right.

Usually when a Patient moves down to a Unit his contact with us is limited, but in your case, we need to continue to see you.

Okay.

For the next week, you'll need to come up here a twice a day, after breakfast and dinner, to get your antibiotics and your Librium. What I'm giving you is your last dose of Diazepam.

Got it.

He looks at my mouth.

We're taking you to a Dentist tomorrow.

I haven't looked at my mouth yet.

He knows what he's doing and he's a friend of mine. He'll take good care of you.

I'm scared to see myself.

Stay strong and you'll be fine.

Scared of the hate that my own image can conjure.

You should get changed and go wait in the Lounge.

All right.

They'll send someone up from the Unit to get you.

I can't wait.

He laughs and he stands up.

Good luck, James.

I stand.

Thank you.

We shake hands and he leaves and I change into the clothes he brought me. A pair of khakis, a white T-shirt, some slippers. They're warm and soft and they feel good. I almost feel human.

I leave my Room and I walk through the Medical Unit, where nothing has changed. There are bright lights, there is whiteness. There are Patients and Doctors and lines and pills. There are moans and screams. There is sadness, insanity and ruin. I know these things and they no longer affect me. I walk into the Lounge and I sit down on a couch. I'm alone and I watch television and the latest batch of pills kicks in.

My heart beat slows.

My hands stop shaking.

My eyelids drop.

My body is limp.

Nothing registers.

I hear my name and I look up and Lilly is standing in front of me. She smiles and she sits down next to me.

Remember me?

Lilly.

She smiles.

I wasn't sure you would. You look pretty juiced.

Librium and Diazepam.

Yeah, I just got off it. I hate that shit.

It's better than nothing.

She laughs.

Talk to me in a couple days.

I smile.

I doubt I'm gonna last a couple of days.

She nods.

I know the feeling.

I don't respond. She speaks.

Where you from?

I reach for my cigarettes.

North Carolina.

I draw one out.

Got one of those for me?

I hand her a cigarette and I light them and we smoke and Lilly tells me about herself and I listen to her. She's twenty-two and grew up in Phoenix. Her Father left when she was four and her Mother was a Heroin Addict who supported her

I open the front passenger door of the Van and I jump inside and the Van is running and it is warm. There is an old weather-beaten jacket similar to the one Hank is wearing sitting on the seat. I pick it up and put it on and settle in and clutch myself. After a few seconds, Hank, who did not need to run, opens the driver's door and climbs in.

You found the coat.

It was hard to miss.

I used to wear it when I worked on my boat.

It has that look.

It's a good coat.

It's working great right now.

I know you don't have one, or have anything from what I'm told, so I want you to use it while you're here.

Thank you, Hank. I appreciate that.

Don't mention it.

I really appreciate it. Thank you.

Don't mention it.

Hank puts the Van into gear and we pull away from the Clinic and we start making our way toward Town. Hank concentrates on the road and I stare out the window and I think. A few days ago the land was shutting down and preparing for winter and dying. Now it's shut down and prepared and dead. There are no leaves on the trees, no living vegetation on the ground, not an insect or a bird or an animal in sight. The thunder is getting louder and closer and the sleet is getting harder and faster and the wind is trying to push the Van into a ditch. Hank keeps it on the road. I stare out the window and I think.

I knew the facts within a month of first laying eyes on her. She was from Connecticut, her Father was a prominent investment banker in New York, her Mother played tennis and bridge and was the President of the local Junior League. She had gone to a prestigious all-girls prep school in New Hampshire. She had an older Brother and an older Sister. She had never had a boyfriend.

I met her when a friend of mine asked me if I could get him some dope. He wasn't a smoker so I asked him who wanted it and he told me it was for a girl named Lucinda who lived in his dorm and I told him I would have to meet her first so he gave me the Room number and I went to the Room and I knocked on the door and the door opened and she was standing there. Tall and thin, long blond hair like thick ropes of silk, eyes cut from the Arctic. I didn't know Lucinda and I didn't know she lived with Lucinda and I couldn't speak and she was standing there. She was standing there.

Hi.

I just stared.

Can I help you with something?

I started to open my mouth and my mouth didn't work and my heart was pounding and my hands were shaking and I felt dizzy and excited and scared and insignificant. She was standing in front of me. Right in front of me. Tall and thin, long blond hair like thick ropes of silk, eyes cut from the Arctic.

I turned and I walked away without a word. I didn't look back and I went to my Room and I got a strong bottle and I took a strong drink. My heart was still pounding and my hands were still shaking and for the first time in my life it wasn't because of alcohol or drugs and for the first time in my life alcohol and drugs wouldn't make it go away.

We pull into town and it is empty. There are no parked cars, no shoppers, no young Mothers walking with Children, no old men on benches with coffee and words of wisdom. The Stores are open, but they're not doing business. The only things out are thunder and sleet and wind. They are getting stronger.

We park in the same spot in front of the same Building and Hank turns off the Van and reaches over and opens the glove compartment and removes two old, yellow tennis balls. He hands them to me.

I thought you might want these.

Why?

I don't know much about anything except for fishing and driving, but I have a feeling whatever you're getting done this morning is gonna hurt.

Probably.

You're not gonna get painkillers or anesthesia, at least not while you're still a Patient at a Treatment Center. I've found the next best things is those balls. When it starts hurting, start squeezing.

I hold the balls in my hand, give them a squeeze.

Thanks.

Sure.

He opens his door and he gets out and I do the same and we shut the doors and we walk into the Building and we walk up the stairs to the Dentist's Office. The door is open and we go inside and I sit on one of the couches in the Waiting Room and Hank goes to Reception and he starts talking to the Receptionist. The Babar the Elephant book is sitting in front of me. I pick it up and start reading it. I remember reading it as a small Boy and enjoying it and imagining that I was friends with Babar, his constant Companion during all of his adventures. He went to the Moon, I went with him. He fought Tomb Raiders in Egypt, I fought alongside him. He rescued his elephant girlfriend from Ivory Hunters on the Savanna, I coordinated the getaway. I loved that goddamn Elephant and I loved being his friend. In a childhood full of unhappiness and rage, Babar is one of the few pleasant memories that I have. Me and Babar, kicking some motherfucking ass.

Hank comes back and he sits down next to me.

They're ready for you.

All right.

You ready for them?

I hold up the tennis balls.

Yeah.

It'll be interesting to see what you look like with teeth.

It'll be interesting to have them again.

I stand.

I'll see you in a while, Hank. Thanks for everything.

Don't mention it.

I walk toward a door where a Nurse stands waiting for me. As I walk past her she is careful not to touch me and I am brought back from the happy afterglow of pachyderm memories and I am reminded of what I am. I am an Alcoholic and I am a drug Addict and I am a Criminal. I am missing my front four teeth. I have a hole in my cheek that has been closed with forty-one stitches. I have a broken nose and I have black swollen eyes. I have an Escort because I am a Patient at a Drug and Alcohol Treatment Center. I am wearing a borrowed jacket because I don't have one of my own. I am carrying two old yellow tennis balls because I'm not allowed to have any painkillers or anesthesia. I am an Alcoholic. I am a drug Addict. I am a Criminal. That's what I am and I don't blame the Nurse for not wanting to touch me. If I weren't me, I wouldn't want to touch me.

She leads me into a small Room. The Room is like many other Rooms I have been in lately, except that it seems cleaner and whiter. There are stainless steel cabinets along the walls, trays of sharp sparkling instruments on top of the cabinets, a large halogen lamp hanging from the ceiling. There is a surgical chair sitting in the middle of the floor. It is metal and it has green cushions and long menacing arms and all sorts of straps and buttons and levers and gears. It looks like a medieval torture device. I know it is for me. I walk past the Nurse and I sit down in the chair and I try to make myself comfortable but it's not possible. Torture devices are not made to be comfortable.

Doctor Stevens will be here in a minute.

All right.

Can I get you anything while you wait?

A Babar book.

Excuse me?

I would like a Babar the Elephant book. You have them in the Waiting Room.

I'll be right back.

Thank you.

She leaves and I'm alone and as I settle into the chair and look around the Room, I start to panic. The last of the Librium is nearly gone and the food in my stomach has been broken down to the point that it no longer holds and everything speeds up. My heart, my blood pressure, the thoughts in my head. My hands are shaking, but it is not the heavy shaking of withdrawal. It is a quick and fragile form of shaking, a form of shaking that comes from fear. Fear of this Room, fear of the chair, fear of what the cabinets hold, fear of what the instruments do, fear of what's going to happen to me here, fear of a pain so great that I need to squeeze tennis balls to make it go away.

The Nurse returns with the Babar book and she gives it to me and she leaves. I set the tennis balls in my lap and I open the book and I try to read it. As I turn the pages, I can see the words and I can see the pictures but I can't read the words and I can't understand the pictures. Everything is speeding up. My heart, my blood pressure, the thoughts in my head. I can't concentrate on anything. Not even Babar.

I close the book and I clutch it against my chest and wait. Everything is shaking. My hands, my feet, the muscles in my legs, my chest, my jaw, my remaining teeth. I pick up the balls and I squeeze them and I try to force the strength of the shaking into the balls and the balls start shaking. Everything is shaking.

The door opens and the Lumberjack Dentist Doctor Stevens walks in and he is followed by another Dentist and two female Nurses. Doctor Stevens pulls up a stainless steel stool and he sits down on the stool near the bottom of the chair. The other Dentist and the Nurses begin collecting bins and instruments and opening cabinet doors and closing cabinet doors. The noises they are making are sharp and I don't know what exactly they are doing but I know the sum of it will be going into my mouth.

Hi, James.

Hi.

Sorry for the wait. We were reviewing the procedures we're going to do today.

No problem.

The other Dentist leans down and whispers something in Doctor Stevens's ear. Doctor Stevens nods. The sum of it will be going into my mouth.

The first thing we want to do is cap the outside two teeth. We looked at the X rays again and the roots seem to be intact, the bases stable. Once they're capped, they should be fine.

Okay.

After we do that, we need to do root-canal surgery on the middle two. The roots are unstable and if we don't do the surgery, your teeth will turn black and die. After they die, they will fall out. I'm assuming you don't want that to happen.

No, I don't.

I'm sorry to be so blunt.

I appreciate your bluntness.

I want you to know exactly what we're doing and why.

I don't want to know any more.

There is one thing.

What?

This is going to be incredibly painful. Because you're currently a Patient at a Drug Treatment Center, we can't use any anesthesia, local or general, and when we're done, we can't give you any painkillers.

I hold up the balls, give them a light squeeze.

I know.

And you think you can deal with that?

I've been through worse.

What?

I've been through worse.

Doctor Stevens stares at me as if what I have said is incomprehensible to him. I know what I'm about to experience is going to be horrible and I don't know if I've been through anything worse, but in order to do this, I have to believe that I have. I stare back.

Let's go, Doc. Bring it.

He stands and begins talking in hushed tones to the other Dentist and to the Nurses and he helps them prepare the bins and instruments for their use in my mouth. I sit and wait and my body slows down and my mind slows down and I stop shaking and I stop squeezing the balls and I am calm. I have accepted that this is going to happen and that I need it to happen and that it's going to hurt. A calm descends, a calm the Condemned must experience just before Execution.

Doctor Stevens steps forward and stands over me.

I'm going to lean you back a bit.

Okay.

He reaches down and he pulls a lever and he slowly and gently leans me back. The halogen light is directly over me and it is blinding in its brightness and I close my eyes. I am holding the balls and the Babar book is resting on my chest, just above my heart.

Do you mind if I move this book?

I'd rather you didn't.

That's fine. We'll work around it.

I hear the shuffling of feet and the placement of bins and someone lifts my head and places the strings of a bib around the back of my neck and clips them and places the bib on top of the book. The chair moves farther down and farther back and a small firm pillow is placed beneath the base of my skull.

A female voice. A clinical manner.

I need you to open your mouth.

I open my mouth.

If it hurts, say so.

Okay.

Now stay still.

I stay still as someone's hand pulls my bottom lip out and stuffs the space between my lip and gum with cotton. I can feel the stitches stretch and blood

59

fire escape and destroyed face. Checked into Treatment Center. Left Treatment Center. Died two days later. Fatal dosage levels of alcohol and cocaine found in system. Death ruled accidental overdose. Should have been ruled suicide. Intentional Suicide. He is survived by no one. His Family had written him off, his friends had written him off.

My mind is clear and my urges are gone and my heart is beating slow and steady. In my mind, my obituary is done. It is done and it is right. It tells the truth, and as awful as it can be, the truth is what matters. It is what I should be remembered by, if I am remembered at all. Remember the truth. It is all that matters.

My mind is clear and my urges are gone and my heart is beating slow and steady. I have made my decision and I am comfortable with my decision. It's what I always knew would happen, though the details are just now coming into focus. I am going to leave here and I am going to kill myself. I am going to leave here and I am going to find something to drink and I am going to find something to smoke and I am going to drink and smoke until I die. I am going to leave here and I'm not going to look back and I'm not going to say good-bye. I have lived alone, I have fought alone, I have dealt with pain alone. I will die alone.

I think about when I'm going to leave. I don't want to be seen and I don't want to be followed, I want to disappear quickly and quietly and without any drama, I want as much time in the darkness as I can possibly have. The darkness provides cover, the darkness provides places to hide and the darkness provides comfort. Darkness usually comes around dinner, but dinner would be too obvious. We are required to show up and we are required to eat and though I don't fraternize during dinner, it would be noticed if I were gone. The Lecture follows and the Lecture would be better. People get up and leave during Lectures all the time. They get up and go to the Bathroom, head outside for a smoke, leave to meet with a Counselor or a Shrink, run to get sick. It would not be noticed if I left, and by the time anyone realized I was gone, which would probably be three or four hours later, I would be far enough away that there would be no bringing me back. I would be in the darkness. I would be alone. I would be comfortable. There would be no bringing me back.

My mind is clear and my urges are gone and my heart is beating slow and steady. I am going to leave here and I am going to kill myself. The thought makes me smile. It makes me smile because it is sad and horrible. It makes me smile because the mystery of my death is gone and without the mystery it isn't scary anymore. It makes me smile because I would rather smile than cry. It makes me smile because it's going to be over. It is finally going to be over. It is finally going to be over. Thank you.

I take a deep breath and I wonder how many breaths I have left. I feel my heart beat and I wonder how many more. I run my hands along my body and my body is warm and soft and I know that soon it will be cold and hard. I feel

my hair, my eyes, my nose, my lips. I feel the whiskers growing on my cheeks.
I touch the skin on my neck, my chest, my arms. It will all be rotting soon.
Decomposing and disintegrating. Disappearing. Every trace will cease to exist.
Ashes to ashes, dust to dust. We return from which we came. I will be rotting
and decomposing and disintegrating soon.

I hear the door open and I sit up. Roy and Lincoln walk in. Roy is smirking
and Lincoln looks pissed. Lincoln speaks.

What are you doing?

Sitting here.

Why aren't you in group?

I needed some time alone.

You should have told somebody.

I didn't feel like telling anybody.

Things here aren't always about what you feel like doing.

If you're here to bitch at me about group, I'll go right now. If you're here to
bitch about something else, let's get it over with.

Lincoln turns to Roy.

Roy.

Roy steps forward.

You didn't clean the Group Toilets this morning.

I laugh. Roy looks at Lincoln. Lincoln speaks.

What's so funny?

His dumb-ass attempt to get me in trouble.

Roy speaks.

I'm not attempting anything. You didn't clean the Group Toilets this morning.

I laugh again.

Fuck you, Roy.

Roy looks at Lincoln. Lincoln looks at me.

They're not clean, James. He just showed them to me.

I look at him.

I cleaned them at about four o'clock this morning. Cleaned them till they fucking sparkled. If they're dirty now it's because somebody used them or somebody,
most likely him, fucked them up to get me in trouble.

Roy speaks.

Not true.

I laugh.

Fuck you, Roy.

He turns to Lincoln. Whines like a spoiled little boy.

It's not true.

Lincoln speaks.

Whether they were clean earlier is irrelevant. It's your job to keep them
clean all the time and right now they're dirty as hell. You need to go clean
them again.

No way.

Absolutely yes.

No fucking way.

Right now.

You're fucking crazy if you think I'm gonna touch those toilets. I cleaned them earlier and Roy fucked them up to get me in trouble. Let Roy clean the god-damn things this time.

Lincoln steps forward, I lean against the back of the bed. He looms over me, puts on his fighting face.

You're going to clean them whether you want to or not and you're going to do it right now and you're not going to say another word about it. You understand me?

I push myself off the bed and I stand and I stare him in the eye.

You gonna force me?

I stare him in the eye.

You gonna try to force me?

I stare him in the eye.

Come on, Lincoln. What are you gonna do?

We stare at each other, breathe slow, clench our jaws, wait for a jump. I know nothing is going to happen and that gives me the advantage. I know that if he touches me he'll lose his job. I know the job is too important to him to risk for me. I know he's gotten soft after years of sobriety and I know that at this point, the black clothes and the boots and the haircut are little more than a costume. I know nothing is going to happen and that he has taken this so far is humor-ous to me. I laugh in his face. He speaks.

This is not a laughing matter.

I laugh again.

I'm not cleaning your fucking toilets, Tough Guy. No fucking way.

I step around him.

James.

I start to leave.

No fucking way.

I walk past Roy and I walk out of the room and I go to the Upper Level of the Unit and I drink a cup of coffee and I smoke a couple of cigarettes and the nicotine and the caffeine feel good inside of me. They speed up my heart, slow down my brain, settle my hands, jump-start my feet. They are strong enough so that I can feel their effects, but not strong enough to really do anything sig-nificant. I like them and I like the combination they form. One speedy and manic, the other slow and depressing. They ebb and flow so that I experience them on both ends of the spectrum. Fast as I can go, low as I can go, every-thing in between. It's fun playing with the doses and the levels and it's fun ma-nipulating the buzz. It's like firing a gun at a target. I get the feeling and I get the rush and I get the experience, but there's no danger. I am in complete control of what I'm doing and what I'm feeling. As in a gunfight, I know that when I switch to the real thing there will be no controlling anything. No fucking way. As much as I can as fast as I can. Till I die.

Men begin filing in from their groups and heading to the Dining Hall for lunch. I follow them and I eat with Leonard. He asks me a lot of questions and I don't answer any of them. He thinks it's funny and I think it's funny and at a certain point he gives up and he tells me stories about our fellow Patients. They are all the same. Had it all, got fucked up, lost it all. Trying to recover. The Great American Sob Story.

After lunch we go to the Lecture, which is about exercise and sobriety. I don't listen to a single word of it, don't care one fucking bit, and Leonard throws pennies at the Bald Man who is now my Roommate. He aims for his head and he gets excited when he hits the center of the bald spot on the top of the man's skull. For some reason the man tolerates it.

The Lecture ends and we go back to the Unit and I attend my first Group Therapy Session. The topic is amends. The group is led by Ken and they discuss the necessity of making amends. Ken believes they are imperative, as do most of the men in the group. Making them allows one to start with a clean slate, to get rid of the guilt Addicts accrue with their actions, to shed the skin of their previous life. Whether they are accepted or not isn't important. What is important is the act of apologizing, the act of admitting fault, the act of asking for forgiveness.

The men who don't believe in amends are the worst of the group. They know that most of what they have done shouldn't be forgiven and won't be forgiven. They don't want to make the effort of asking because the pain of rejection and the reminder of their actions will hurt too much. They want to move on and forget, even though forgetting is impossible. I am in their class. I know I won't be forgiven and I'm not going to bother to ask. My amends will be my death. No one I have hurt will ever have to see me, hear from me, or think about me ever again. I won't be able to damage them or fuck up their lives anymore, I won't be able to cause them the pain I have caused previously. Forget me if you can. Forget I ever existed, forget I did whatever it was I did. My suicide will be my apology. Even though it is impossible, please forget me. Please forget.

After the group all of the men of the Unit gather in the Lower Level and there is a Graduation Ceremony. Roy and his friend are both leaving. They have done their time, worked their Programs and they are ready to rejoin the outside World. They both receive a Medal and a Rock. The Medal signifies their current term of sobriety, the Rock their resolve to stay sober. They both give small speeches. About half of the men despise them and think they're full of shit, the other half admire them and wish them the best. I sit in the back of the Room with Leonard, who reads the *USA Today* sports page and swears under his breath.

The Ceremony ends and everybody claps and Roy walks around giving out hugs and good-byes. He avoids me, as does his friend. They both seem very happy and they both have the glazed eyes of the Converted. They clutch their Medals and their Rocks, have their friends sign the backs of their copies of the *Big Book*. They both look scared and they both look fragile. They both look as if they're running from something and they both look as if they're hiding from something. They both look as if they know they're going to get caught. I give them a month before they're both so fucked up that they can't see straight. I give them a month at best.

Most of the men head to their Rooms and start getting ready for dinner. I head to mine to get ready to leave. I take off Warren's oxford and put on my T-shirt and I write Warren a note of thanks and I put it in the front pocket of the oxford and I walk over to his area and I fold the oxford and I set it on his bed. I go back to my area and I write another note that has Hank's name and the address of the Clinic and says Please Return This Jacket and thanks Hank for his kindness and friendship. I put this note in the front pocket of the jacket he lent me so it will be found when I am found and I put the jacket on and I look around for anything else I might have, but there's nothing. I look in the drawers, on the bed, under the bed, under the sheets, in the medicine cabinet, in the shower. There is nothing. I have nothing.

I walk to the Dining Hall and I get in line and I grab a tray and I take a deep breath and the smell of the food floods my body and I am hungry, hungry, hungry and I want to eat and I want to eat a lot. Tonight's meal is meat loaf and mashed potatoes and gravy and brussels sprouts and apple pie. It is a meal I like and it is suitable for what will probably be the last real meal that I eat. I get as much as the woman behind the counter will give me and I get utensils and napkins and I find an empty table and I sit down and I spread the napkins on my lap and I take a deep breath. This is probably going to the last real meal I ever eat.

The meat loaf is good and wet and juicy and the potatoes are real potatoes and the gravy is warm and thick and tastes deeply of beef. I eat slowly, savoring each bite, letting each bite sit in my mouth until it dissolves. My Mother made meat loaf for my Brother and me when I was a Child, made this exact meal about once a week. Eating it now and eating it as my last meal brings back the memories of those dinners and of many more. My Father would be working or away somewhere on some trip, my Brother and I would be at School or running around whatever neighborhood we happened to live in at the time. At six-thirty every night, we'd have dinner with my Mother. She made great dinners, and she loved the routine of sitting down and eating with us. After dinner we'd watch television or play games or my Mother would read to us. When my Father made it home we would spend time together as a whole and then it was off to bed for my Brother and me. We were a Family, a happy Family, and we stayed that way until I stopped showing up. It would be nice to have my Family here with me now. It would be nice, despite the disintegration of our relationship over the past years, to have a final dinner with them. Though I doubt we would talk much, it would be nice to look each of them in the eye and say good-bye to them. Though I doubt we would talk much, it would be nice to hold each of their hands, tell them that I'm sorry, that me being who I am wasn't their fault. Though I doubt we would talk much, I would like to tell them to forget me.

I finish eating and I lean back in my chair and I see Leonard walking toward me with a tray of food. He sets down his tray on the table and he sits across from me and he starts unfolding napkins and cleaning his silverware.

How are ya, Kid?

I'm good.

You're good?

Yeah, I'm good.

That's the first time I ever heard you say that.

I'm coming to terms with some shit.

What?

None of your business.

One of these days you're gonna talk to me.

No, I'm not.

You'll get tired of being an Asshole and you'll get tired of not having any friends and you'll talk to me.

No, I won't.

I'm gonna keep sitting with you until you do.

I laugh.

I'm gonna keep sitting with you. Mark my motherfucking words.

I grab my tray, stand.

Have a nice life, Leonard.

What's that supposed to mean?

Have a nice life.

I turn and I walk my tray to the conveyor and I drop it on the belt and I start to walk out of the Dining Hall. As I head through the Glass Corridor separating the men and women, I see Lilly sitting alone at a table. She looks up at me and she smiles and our eyes meet and I smile back. She looks down and I stop walking and I stare at her. She looks up and she smiles again. She is as beautiful a girl as I have ever seen. Her eyes, her lips, her teeth, her hair, her skin. The black circles beneath her eyes, the scars I can see on her wrists, the ridiculous clothes she wears that are ten sizes too big, the sense of sadness and pain she wears that is even bigger. I stand and I stare at her, just stare stare stare. Men walk past me and other women look at me and Lilly doesn't understand what I'm doing or why I'm doing it and she's blushing and it's beautiful. I stand there and I stare. I stare because I know where I am going I'm not going to see any beauty. They don't sell crack in Mansions or fancy Department Stores and you don't go to luxury Hotels or Country Clubs to smoke it.

thank him. Andy tells me he found me knocked out and bleeding and he carried me to a car and took me to the Hospital. He begged the Doctor not to call the Police and he begged the Doctor to put me on a plane. He called my Parents and he took me to the Airport and he got me on the Plane. I thank him and I tell him that if I happen to be saved that he will partially be responsible for saving me. He tells me it's no big deal and he tells me that he would do it again if he needed to do it again, but he hopes that he doesn't. I ask him if he knows what I was on or what I was doing in Ohio and he tells me that he found a crack pipe in my pocket and he saw a bloody tube of glue a few feet from where he found me, but beyond that, he doesn't know anything. He had heard I had shown up at ten in the morning and that I was drunk and incoherent and I had disappeared for the day. The first time he saw me was when he found me on the ground. I thank him again. We say good-bye. We hang up.

I call my Parents. My Mother answers the phone and she accepts the call.

James.

She sounds frantic.

Hi, Mom.

Let me get your Father.

She holds the phone away, yells for my Father. He picks up.

How are you, James?

I'm fine, Dad.

You're doing okay?

I'm fine.

My Mother speaks.

Are you getting better?

I don't know.

Do you feel any better?

I don't know.

Are you learning anything?

I don't know.

She exhales, exhales frustration. My Father speaks.

James.

Yeah.

Your Mom and I have been talking to some of the Counselors up there and we want to come see you.

No.

Why?

Because I don't want you here.

Why?

Because I don't.

My Mother speaks.

They have something called the Family Program where we would spend three days learning about your sickness and learning about how to help you deal with it. We'd like to come do it.

My sickness?

Alcoholism and Drug Addiction is a disease, James.

Who told you that?

It's in all the books.

Right. The books.

There is an uncomfortable pause. Father speaks.

We'd really like to do the Program, James. We think it could be really good for all of us.

I don't want you here, and if you come, I'll be fucking pissed.

My Mother speaks.

Could you please not swear.

I'll try.

Another uncomfortable pause. I speak.

Go back to Tokyo. I'll call you next week to tell you how I'm doing.

My Father speaks.

We're very worried about you, James.

I hear my Mother start to cry.

I know you are.

We really want to come up there.

Cry.

Do what you want, but don't expect me to participate if you do.

Do you need anything?

Cry.

I need to go.

We love you, James.

I know you do.

My Mother speaks.

I love you, James.

Her voice breaks.

I know you do, Mom.

My Father speaks.

Call us if we can help in any way.

I've got to go, Dad.

Please reconsider the Family Program.

Bye, Dad.

Bye, James.

My Mother sobs.

Bye, James.

Bye, Mom.

My Mother sobs.

We love you.

I've got to go.

I hang up the phone and I take a deep breath and I stare at the floor. My Mother and Father are at a House in Michigan that I've never seen and my Mother is crying and my Father is trying to comfort her and their hearts are broken and they want to come see me and they want to try to help me and I don't want them here and I don't want their help. My Mother is crying because her Son is an Alcoholic and a drug Addict and a Criminal. My Father is trying to comfort her. I have broken their hearts. I stare at the floor.

I walk back to my Room and I sit down on my bed. John is in his area and when he sees me he stands and walks toward my area.

I'm sorry for giving your friend my card.

I'm not mad at you.

It's okay if you are.

We thought it was funny.

I figured out a way to make it better.

I'm not mad.

Let me make it better.

There's nothing to make better.

Please.

He sits down at the edge of my bed, gives me an earnest look.

How old are you?

Twenty-three.

You're so young.

I chuckle.

What's your offer, John?

He takes a deep breath.

This is to make up for all my wrongs.

Okay.

And if it's not sufficient, we can talk about something else.

What's the offer, John?

He reaches into his pocket, pulls out a picture, hands it to me. It is of a beautiful young Girl in a bikini.

What's this?

My Daughter.

She's beautiful, but I don't want a picture of your Daughter.

That's not it.

Then what is it?

I want to give her to you. You can do whatever you want to her.

Goddamn, John.

I hand him the picture.

You don't like her?

You can't give me your fucking Daughter.

My Family supports her and pays all of her and her Mother's bills.

So what.

She'll do what I say.

Go away, John.

She'll do anything I say.

Then tell her to go to School, stay away from drugs and stay the fuck away from you.

That's good advice.

Go away, John.

I'm sorry.

Don't be sorry, John. Just go away.

He stands.

Okay.

He walks to his section of the room and he climbs into bed and he buries himself under the covers and I can hear him cursing himself. He's a poor, sick, sad Motherfucker, but once he was an innocent young Boy. A Boy with a future, a Boy with his whole life in front of him. His Dad was rich and powerful, and one day, one horrible fucked-up day, his Dad decided to molest him. I can imagine young John, alone in his room with a set of army men or stack of Legos or a pile of baseball cards, and I can imagine his Dad coming in and shutting the door and telling John he wanted some private time with him. After it was over, I can imagine John crawling into his bed and burying himself under the covers and cursing himself.

I sit and I listen to John crying and I wish there was something I could do to help him. I sit and I listen to John and I wish there was some way I could make him better. There is no hope for John, no hope at all. He could go to five hundred Clinics and spend ten years working the Twelve Steps and it wouldn't make a bit of fucking difference. He has been broken beyond repair, wounded beyond the point of healing, abused beyond the point of recovery. He will never know happiness or joy, security or normalcy. He will never know pleasure, satisfaction, serenity, clarity, peace of mind or any semblance of sanity. He will never know trust or love. You poor, sick, sad Motherfucker. You will never know. I'm sorry.

I hear voices and activity outside the door to the Room and I know that it is time for dinner. I walk over to John's area and sit down on a chair next to his bed. He is still under the covers, still mumbling and cursing, still thrashing and still punching himself.

John?

He stops, lies still.

John?

Still.

John?

What do you want?

It's time for dinner.

I don't want to eat dinner.

What are you gonna do?

Stay here.

That's stupid.

Go away.

Get out from under there and come have dinner.

Go away.

I'm not leaving until you do.

Go away.

No.

He throws the covers off of himself and he stares at me with his hardest look. I laugh at him.

What's so funny?

Your Tough Guy look isn't very tough.

I'm tougher than you think.

Yeah, you probably are, but you sure don't look it.

He changes his face into a strange grimace and snarls. I laugh at him again.

That's not any better.

It's not?

No.

He relaxes, looks normal.

I wanna be alone.

Being alone won't do any good for you, John.

I wanna be alone.

It's better to be around people. It makes it hurt less.

How do you know?

I know.

No you don't.

Trust me, I do.

John looks at me, looks down at his blanket.

Come on, let's go.

He looks up.

It hurts a lot, James.

I know it does.

I wish it would go away.

I know the feeling.

What do you do?

Deal with it, and hope someday that you don't have to anymore.

He looks down.

Yeah.

He looks up and he swings his legs off the bed and he stands and I stand and we walk out of the Room. We walk into the Unit and we get in the back of a line. The food has been delivered and set up on a table on the Upper Level. The line runs from the table down the stairs that lead to the Lower Level. As the line moves forward, and as I get closer to the food, the smell ignites my hunger. I want to eat and I want to eat immediately and I want to eat until I explode. I want want want want. Fuel. Right fucking now.

As I begin to climb the stairs, my hunger and my need begin to overwhelm me. My hands start shaking, my heart rate increases, I'm nervous, anxious and angry. I stare at the food. I don't see or hear or smell anything else. Each second is an hour long, each step a marathon. I want, want, want, want. Fuel. Right fucking now. I would kill if somebody tried to take the food away, I would kill if somebody tried to stop me from getting to it. Need need need need need.

I reach the end of the table, pick up a plate, stuff a plastic knife and a plastic fork and a paper napkin in my pocket. The food is on trays and in bowls and a man from the Restaurant is serving it and Leonard is standing next to him supervising. He asks me what I want and I say everything. He asks me what part of the turducken I like and I tell him I don't know what a turducken is and I don't care what it is, I just want a lot of it. Leonard laughs at me as I ask for more and more and more. I could give a shit about him right now. I want need fuel now.

I sit down on a couch next to John and I pull the fork out of my pocket and I try to use it but my hand is shaking too much to use it so I start shoveling food into my mouth with my fingers. I don't look at it, I don't taste it, I chew it enough so that I can swallow it. It is not important to experience it or enjoy it. It is important to fill. That is all I want out of this meal. Enough to fill.

I finish my plate and I get another one. I finish that plate and I get another one. I finish that plate and I get another one. I finish that plate. I am beyond full, beyond stuffed. I have moved beyond need and into abuse and I am comfortable. My heart and my hands are slowing down, my senses and the ability to think are returning, the nerves, anxiety and anger are fading away. Beyond need and into abuse. It is nice to be comfortable. It is nice to be Home.

I take a deep breath. I can feel my stomach stretching. I know it's not going to stretch enough. It hasn't come yet, but it will. It will come fast and hard.

I stand and John asks me where I'm going and I tell him that I'll be right back and I start walking back to the Room. I walk up the stairs, through the Upper Level, down a short Hall. As I open the door, it starts to come. Hard and fast. I'm twenty feet from the toilet.

It comes and I keep my mouth closed and I breathe through my nose. I didn't

talks about drinking and drugs. When he talks of heroin, he taps the bend of his elbow with two fingers, when he talks of coke he sniffs, booze he makes a motion like he has a bottle, pills as if he's tossing them in. He claims that at the height of his use he would do five thousand dollars of cocaine and heroin a day mixed with four to five fifths of booze a night and up to forty pills of Valium to sleep. He says this with complete sincerity and with the utmost seriousness.

I am tired and I am spent. I am nervous and I am happy. I am calm. Were I in my normal frame of mind, I would stand up, point my finger, scream Fraud, and chase this Chump Motherfucker down and give him a beating. Were I in my normal frame of mind, after I gave him his beating, I would make him come back here and apologize to everyone for wasting their precious time. After the apology, I would tell him that if I ever heard of him spewing his bullshit fantasies in Public again, I would cut off his precious hair, scar his precious lips, and take all of his goddamn gold records and shove them straight up his ass.

I don't like this man. I don't like what he has to say or how he's saying it. I don't believe him and his Rock Star status isn't enough to make me buy the shit he's trying to sell. Four to five thousand dollars a day of anything is enough to kill a Person several times over. Five bottles of strong liquor over the course of a night would render the strongest human on Earth comatose. Forty Valiums to sleep and he'd take a fucking nap from which he'd never return. He'd never return and maybe that would be best.

An Addict is an Addict. It doesn't matter whether the Addict is white, black, yellow or green, rich or poor or somewhere in the middle, the most famous Person on the Planet or the most unknown. It doesn't matter whether the addiction is drugs, alcohol, crime, sex, shopping, food, gambling, television, or the fucking Flintstones. The life of the Addict is always the same. There is no excitement, no glamour, no fun. There are no good times, there is no joy, there is no happiness. There is no future and no escape. There is only an obsession. An all-encompassing, fully enveloping, completely overwhelming obsession. To make light of it, brag about it, or revel in the mock glory of it is not in any way, shape or form related to its truth, and that is all that matters, the truth. That this man is standing in front of me and everyone else in this room lying to us is heresy. The truth is all that matters. This is fucking heresy.

The Lecture ends and there is wild applause and enthusiastic cheers and the Lips, Hair, Leather and Silk on the Stage is smiling and waving and glowing and blowing kisses to his adoring Fans. I am tired. I am spent. I am nervous and I am happy and I am calm. Were I in my normal frame of mind, I'd be sick to my stomach. I hear Leonard mumbling and I ask him what he just said and he laughs and tells me that he's thinking of sending a few of his Associates to have a talk with the Lips about an attitude adjustment. I laugh and I tell him it would be a beautiful thing. Bless you, Leonard. It would be a beautiful fucking thing.

We stand and we start to file out and before I leave I turn to get a glimpse of Lilly but I can't see her and I don't want to make my intentions obvious so I turn back and I keep walking. I wish I could see her. I want to see her. I don't see her. I walk back to the Unit and I go to my Room and I lie down on my bed.

Miles walks in and he sits down on his bed and he reaches for his clarinet case and he starts unpacking it and he asks if I mind if he plays and I say no play whatever you want for as long as you want and I reach for a book one of the books my Brother gave me and I don't bother looking to see what I'm reaching for because I don't care I just want to read and I want to occupy my mind with something. The rage and need are back they have returned are alive as they almost always are living and lingering and eating me away. I need something to occupy my mind. I don't care what it is. Occupy.

I pull the Chinese book, the *Tao te Ching*, by far the smallest of the three that I have, and the only one that I haven't read before. It is a small, thin paperback. The title is written across the front in simple white type against a black background. I flip the book over and I look at the back and there are quotes on the back from three sources that I have never heard of before but that look like bullshit new-age Hippie Periodicals. There is a publication classification in an upper corner. It reads Religion.

I am immediately skeptical. Not only because of the source quotes and the Religion classification, but because I've always grouped books such as this in a category with crap like Astrology, Aromatherapy, Crystalology, Pyramid Power, Psychic Healing and Feng Shui, which at various times in my life have all been suggested as cures for my problems. That anyone would actually believe that these things could solve their problems, really solve them, instead of just making them forget about them for a while, is asinine to me. My Brother gave me this book though, so I'll read it. Had anyone aside from my Brother given it to me, it would be sitting in the bottom of a garbage can.

As I open it, Miles starts playing his clarinet. He plays softly and slowly. The notes are on the low side and he draws them out to the point that I wonder how he's breathing. The notes are on the long side and he makes them sound like they are easy to make, though I know they are not. Low and slow and soft and long and easy. I don't know what it is, but I like it.

I skip the Introduction. If the book goes in the trash, I want it to go because of my thoughts on it, not because of some Asshole's thoughts who wrote the Introduction.

The text begins. It consists of a series of short poems numbered one through eighty-one. The first one says that the Tao is that which has no name and is beyond any sort of name. It says that names are not necessary for that which is real and for that which is eternal. It says that if we are free from desire, we can realize mystery, that if we are caught in desire, we only realize manifestations. It says mystery and manifestations arise from the same source, which is darkness. It says darkness within darkness is the key to all understanding. It is not enough to make me throw it away, but I am also not convinced.

I keep going. I keep going as I listen to low and slow and soft and long and easy. I keep going as I settle in beneath the warmth of my bed and I keep going as I wait for the phone to ring. When the phone rings, I know I will get to hear the sound of Lilly's voice. I want to hear the sound of Lilly's voice.

Number two. If there is beauty, there is ugliness. If there is good, there is bad. Being and nonbeing and difficult and easy and high and low and long and short and before and after need, depend, create and define each other. Those who live with the Tao act without doing and teach without saying. They let things come and they let things go and they live without possession and they live without expectation. They do not need, depend, create or define. They do not see beauty or ugliness or good or bad. There just is. Just be.

Number three. Overesteem men and people become powerless. Overvalue possessions and people begin to steal. Empty your mind and fill your core. Weaken your ambition and toughen your resolve. Lose everything you know and everything you desire and ignore those who say they know. Practice not wanting, desiring, judging, doing, fighting, knowing. Practice just being. Everything will fall into place.

Four. The Tao is used, but never used up. An eternal void, it is filled with infinite possibilities. It is not there, but always there. It is older and more powerful than any God. It is not there, but always there. It is older and more powerful than any God.

I stop reading and I read them again. One through four, again and again. The words and the words together and the meaning and the context are simple so simple and basic so basic and true and that is all that matters true. They speak to me, make sense to me, reverberate within me, calm ease sedate relax still pacify me. They ring true and that is all that matters the truth. Although I am no expert on this or anything related to this or anything at all except being a fuck-up, I seem to understand what this book this weird beautiful enlightened little book is saying to me. Live and let live, do not judge, take life as it comes and deal with it, everything will be okay.

I close the book and I let the sounds of the clarinet carry me carry me carry me. They are low and slow and soft and long and easy, as are the thoughts in my head. They carry me carry me carry me.

Live and let live.

Do not judge.

Take it as it comes.

Deal with it.

Everything will be okay.

I get Hank's jacket. I put it on and I walk through the Unit. I open one of the glass doors and I step outside. I walk through the grass there is no dew and I find the Trail and I enter the Wood there is Sun streaming through gaps in the trees like girders of light. I walk along the Trail. I see broken branches and I see torn leaves spread like crumbs and the torn leaves lead me. The signs of my destruction lead me.

I push my way through the thick and I step into the Clearing. It is empty. I sit down on the dirt and I lie back and I close my eyes. I have not slept enough and I am tired. I need more sleep I am tired. Tired. I am tired.

I feel a hand on my face. It's soft and warm, resting on my cheek, caressing it without moving. Lips follow it on the other cheek, full and wet and soft and gentle. There is sweet breath behind and sweet breath after. They both leave my cheek I wish they would stay. I open my eyes and I slowly sit up. Lilly is next to me, bundled in a large green Army jacket, black hair in braided pigtails, her pale skin reflecting a girder of Sun. She smiles and she speaks.

Hi.

What time is it?

She looks at a cheap plastic Superwoman watch on her wrist. Beneath it I see scars.

Four-ten.

I rub my face.

I fell asleep.

She smiles again.

I woke you up.

I smile.

I'm glad.

She leans forward and she kisses me on the cheek. She holds her lips soft wet warm and gentle. My instinct is to pull away, but I don't. When she pulls away, she leaves sweet breath behind her.

Answer a question for me.

Okay.

Do you have a Girlfriend?

I hesitate, a flash of her, Arctic and blonde.

No.

Why'd you hesitate?

I did, but I don't anymore. I thought of her for a second.

Where is she?

I have no idea.

When was the last time you spoke to her?

About a year ago.

You over her?

No.

Lilly smiles, leans forward and she kisses my lips.

That's too bad.

I smile. I have no words. If I did have words, they would mean nothing.

You want a smoke?

She reaches into one of the pockets of her jacket and she pulls out a pack of cigarettes.

Yeah.

I take one.

You got a lighter?

I reach into my pocket, pull out a lighter.

Yeah.

I flip it, light her smoke, light mine.

You having a good day?

I inhale. I feel the nicotine immediately. It doesn't feel as good as Lilly's kiss.

It's been long.

She inhales, stares at me.

They're all long in here.

My instinct is to look away, but I don't.

Yeah.

Tell me something.

All right.

Why are you here?

Here at this place or here with you?

Either one.

I don't know.

She smiles.

That's a good answer.

My instinct is to look away, but I don't. I speak.

Why are you here?

She smiles.

Here at this place or here with you?

I smile.

Either.

I came to this place because of my Grandma.

She brought you in?

She convinced me to bring myself in.

How'd she do that?

She loved me and she took care of me even though I was a total disaster, and whenever I did something stupid, which was pretty much every day, she told me that when I was ready to learn about freedom, I should come talk to her. A while back something really, really awful happened. It fucked me up bad and I went and found her and I asked her what she meant. She told me that I was a

Prisoner of my Mom and all of her problems and a Prisoner of my Dad who I don't remember and she told me that I was Prisoner of drugs and sex and of myself. She told me that living life as a Prisoner was a waste of life and that freedom, even a second of freedom, was worth more than a lifetime of bondage. She told me if I wanted to learn more, to come talk to her again the next day. I did, and she told me the same thing. A second of freedom is worth more than a lifetime of bondage. Then she said come back again the next day. I did and she handed me a map and she said let's get in the car, you're driving. Eight hours later that map led me here. She said she had been saving money for three years and if I wanted freedom I should walk in the front doors and she'd pay for it. She said if I didn't, we should drive Home. I hate my life. I have never wanted it to be the way it has been, and this was a chance to escape it. I had heard of this place and knew it was the best place like it and really expensive and I knew if Grandma had saved for me to be here that she wanted it for me and I knew I wanted it as well. To be free, even if it's just for a second. So I walked through the door and here I am.

You free yet?

No, but I'm getting there.

She smiles.

You tell me a story now.

About what?

Tell me about your Girlfriend.

I don't like talking about her.

Why?

Because it hurts too much.

Fair enough. Tell me something else.

Pick something.

How'd you lose your virginity?

Why do you want to know that?

It says a lot about a Person.

It won't say good things about me.

I'm not here to judge you.

Why are you here?

To know you. Or to try.

I stare at her. I stare at her eyes clean water blue and her hair braided jet black. I stare at her skin pale white and her lips blood red, I stare at her body beneath the jacket she is so small. I stare at her wrists and the Superwoman watch and the scars running vertically. I stare at me but not me. I see the damage and pain of hard years. I see the emptiness and desperation of existence without hope. I see a young life that has been too long. I see me but not me. I trust myself. I can trust her.

I've never told anyone this.

You don't have to tell me if you don't want to.

No, I will.

Stop whenever you want.

I stare at her. I see me but not me. I can trust her. I speak.

I was sixteen, a Sophomore in High School. It was Homecoming and there was a Football Game and a Dance. I hated the Town we lived in and my Parents knew I hated it and they felt bad about it. My Mom would always ask me about friends and Girls because she hoped I would meet some People and then I'd be happier. I always lied to her and told her that I had lots of friends and that lots of Girls liked me so that she wouldn't feel so bad. The reality of the situation was that nobody liked me. As this Dance was coming up my Mom kept asking if I was going. I told her I hadn't decided yet, that there were a couple of Girls who wanted to go with me and I wasn't sure which one I liked most and I really just hoped she'd stop asking. She didn't. Every day it was the same. Who are you going to ask, you should decide soon, you need to give the Girl enough time to get ready, it's a special night you shouldn't miss it. Finally I just lied to her and told her I was taking someone. She was really excited and she went out and she got me a suit and she bought me a rose to pin on my lapel and she washed her car and told me I could borrow it and she gave me some money to go out to Dinner before the Game. It fucking sucked because I knew it was all bullshit and I was lying to her.

When the day of the Game came around, I put on the suit and she and my Dad took a bunch of pictures of me and I waved out the car window as I drove away. I parked the car near the School Stadium and I sat and watched all the other Kids, the ones who had dates, as they drove in and hung around in the Stands or on the Sidelines in their suits and dresses and I watched the Halftime Ceremony and I watched the King and Queen get crowned and I watched everyone clap and cheer for them and I watched everyone be happy. When the Game was over, I didn't have anything to do, and I sure wasn't going to go to the Dance alone, so I drove to this Ghetto nearby to try and score some drugs because I felt like shit for lying to my Mom and because I didn't have any friends and I wanted to make the pain go away. As I was driving around, I saw a whore walking on the street near a House where I used to buy. She would stare at me and wave at me as I passed and I couldn't find any drugs so I finally just pulled over. She walked up to the car and asked if I wanted a Date and I said how much and she told me and it was just a little bit less than the money my Mom had given me so I said yes. I don't know why I did it. I guess I was just lonely and sad and hoping to find some sort of love that would make me feel better. What happened was awkward and stupid and disgusting. The woman smelled and talked to me in this fake dirty voice and it was over in about two seconds. I took her back to the street and I drove around for the next couple hours trying to talk myself out of driving full speed into a tree. When I went home I told my Mom and Dad I had a great time and I thanked them for everything they gave me and I went to my

I think that's ridiculous.

Ridiculous things can be true.

Why do your Parents make you so angry?

I don't know.

Did you experience abuse as a child?

Not that I remember.

Do you think it's possible?

No.

Why?

I grew up in a safe, sheltered environment. My Parents have always loved me and they've always tried to protect me and they've always tried to do their best by me. They fucking piss me off, but there is no way they ever abused me.

What about someone else?

No.

Are you sure?

Yes.

I pull a cigarette from my pocket, light it, take a drag. The nicotine slows my heart and calms me.

What next?

Lunch, and after that you go down to the Family Center. You'll spend the afternoon in Group Sessions with the Members of other People's Families until dinner. After dinner, we'll sit down with your Parents again.

Why?

To discuss this morning.

That'll be fun.

You were brave this morning. You were very honest and very straightforward and you said a lot of things that probably weren't easy to say. Your Parents reacted in a very normal, natural way, and if they hadn't reacted that way, I would be worried about our ability to make progress with them. Now that they know what they need to know, we can work on healing your wounds and figuring out how you can get along better.

When will we be done tonight?

Depends on what we get into with your Parents.

Give me an estimate.

You trying to meet up with Lilly?

What?

You heard me.

Yeah, I'm trying to meet up with Lilly.

Don't.

Why?

If you get caught, you'll be in serious trouble.

Sounds like I got caught already.

There is an idea that there is something going on. We have not caught you.

Where'd you get the idea?

I can't discuss that with you.

You want me to discuss things with you, but you won't discuss things with me. That's fucking bullshit, Joanne.

You think so?

Yeah, I do. You be straight with me, I'll be straight with you. That's the fucking deal. If it's not, you can go fuck yourself.

I'm not your enemy.

You are if you're not straight with me.

Lilly is very smitten with you. One of the Counselors on her Unit overheard her talking to one of her Girlfriends about you. She has since heard Lilly talking about you a number of other times. It seems that you're all that Lilly wants to talk about.

I smile.

Why are you smiling?

I like that she's smitten with me.

It's a bad idea, James.

Why?

You should be concentrating on what you're here for, which is getting sober and rebuilding your life. Lilly is a distraction that takes you away from that. Both of you are very fragile and vulnerable right now, and if something went wrong between the two of you, it would jeopardize your sobriety.

I can handle it.

Overconfidence kills a lot of People.

She makes me feel good, better than I feel with anyone else.

I'm sure she does, but that doesn't change our Policy.

I don't want to let her go.

It's in the best of interests of both of you.

I'll take your advice under consideration.

Take it further than that.

I stand.

I'm going to eat.

She nods.

I'll see you tonight.

I turn and I open her door and I walk out of Joanne's Office. I go the Dining Hall. As I walk down the Glass Corridor separating the men from the women, I see Lilly sitting at a table. She is staring at me and I stare back, though I make no other sort of acknowledgment. It is hard to stare at her, hard because she's not the distant Girl who smiles at me anymore. She has become more than that, more than I expected her to become and more than I was looking for her to become. She is becoming what I wanted she the last with the Arctic eyes to become, which is someone who loves me. Simply and truly and as I am. It is hard to stare at her because as I know she is starting to love me, I am starting to love her. I don't care what she's done or who she's done it with, I don't care about whatever demons may be in her closet. I care about how she makes me feel and she makes me feel strong and safe and calm and warm and true. It is hard to stare because I am forced to contemplate giving it up. It is hard to stare, but I do it anyway.

I get a tray and I get in line and I get a plate of tuna noodle casserole. I ask for ten, but the Lady in the hairnet says no. I go to the Salad Bar and I get five plates. I put lettuce on one, cottage cheese on another, beets on the third, niblets of corn on the fourth, croutons on the fifth. My tray is full so I get another tray. I put four plates on it, each piled high with portions of pudding, peaches, slices of apple pie and carrot cake. I walk slowly through the Dining Area carrying both trays. They're heavy and I hear a couple of snickers and I hear a couple of laughs. A voice I don't know says that's a sad addiction. I chuckle. I find my friends Ed and Ted and Leonard and Matty and Miles and I sit down with them. Leonard speaks.

Where you been all day?

My Parents are here.

Miles speaks.

Are they here for the Family Program?

Yeah.

How has it been?

Shitty.

Why?

I had to do this confession thing this morning where I told them about all the bad shit I've done.

Ed speaks.

What didn't they know about?

They didn't know much.

What was the worst?

The crack, and the fact that I'm wanted in three states.

Leonard speaks.

What are you wanted for?

A bunch of shit.

Miles speaks.

Do you have warrants out against you, James?

Yes.

Where?

Michigan, Ohio and North Carolina.

Are you doing anything to take care of them?

Somebody here is trying to do something.

Ted speaks.

When I told my Mamma I smoked the rock she asked if I could get
her some.
Everyone laughs.
She did. She said I been hearing all about this crack stuff and I wanna try me
some. I got a fifty bag and I smoked with her till her eyes were in the back of
her head. She didn't want no more after that.
Everyone laughs again, though the image of Ted's Mamma with her eyes in the
back of her head is not a funny one. We spend the rest of lunch laughing
more, mostly at Matty, who is still struggling to stop swearing. Every third or
fourth word he speaks is either goddamn or fuck and is immediately followed
by a string of other curses which are directed at himself. Eventually he just
stops speaking entirely. By the time lunch is over, the men have devoured the
food on all of my plates everything is gone. As we stand to leave, I look across
the Dining Hall and through the glass at Lilly. She is smiling at me and the
smile hurts. I will not could not don't want to give that smile up. I won't give it
up. No fucking way.
We walk out of the Dining Hall. My friends head toward the Lecture, I walk
through Halls into areas I don't know, following signs that lead me to the
Family Center. I arrive at a door. A sign on the door says Welcome Home. I
open it and I go inside.
The white walls are whiter the lightbulbs brighter the paintings hanging happier. They are filled with scenes of Families on picnics in wide open fields of
green and wildflowers. The members of the Families in the paintings are smiling, eating French bread, cutting fruit and playing backgammon. Variations of
them are along all of the walls. I follow them and they take me to a large open
Room. On one side of the Room, the entire wall is glass and it looks out upon
the Lake. There are chairs in the Room chairs everywhere. Large plush chairs
that look comfortable in their happy patterned upholstery. There are People sitting in the chairs they are talking, smoking, drinking coffee and waiting.
Waiting for their Family Members and waiting to get better.
It is easy to tell who is here as part of the Family Program and who is here as
part of their own Program. The Family Program People wear cleaner clothes
have better haircuts nicer watches sparkling jewelry. Their skin is more flush,
their bodies glow, they have flesh on their bones. They have life in their eyes.
The rest of us smoke cigarettes and drink cups of coffee, our hands shake and
we have bags under our eyes. We move slowly and the only thing alive in our
eyes is dread.
I look around the Room. My Parents are huddled in a corner softly speaking to
each other. They see me. I hold up one finger and my Father nods at me and I
go to the coffee machine. I get a cup, black and steaming, and I walk toward
them.
They stand as I approach. They are smiling and they have changed their

clothes, though the clothes are more or less the same. My Mother has redone her hair and her makeup and it is perfect again and my Father's blazer is crisply pressed. I can see the effort behind their smiles and with each step closer, I want to turn and run. My Father speaks.

How are you, James?

Been better. You?

I think we've been better too.

There is silence, smiling. I wish the smiling would stop. My Mother speaks.

Do you want to sit with us?

I nod, we sit. They are side by side, I am across from them. There is a table between us, it has an ashtray. I reach into my pocket for my cigarettes and I take them out. My Mother frowns.

Could you not smoke, please?

Why?

Because I just changed my clothes and I don't want them to smell.

Fine.

I put the cigarettes back into my pocket. My Mother watches me.

Are you going to quit those things while you're here?

No.

Why?

Because I don't want to quit these things.

Why not?

I'll give you a choice, Mom. I can either smoke cigarettes or smoke crack. You make the call.

She recoils, obviously hurt. I knew it would happen, but I did it anyway. My Father speaks.

I don't think you need to speak to your Mother that way, James. Obviously we'd rather have you smoke cigarettes than smoke crack.

Then don't give me shit about it.

Don't speak to us that way.

I reach for my cup of coffee and I drink it in one gulp. It's hot and steaming and it burns my mouth, but I don't care. I pull the cup away and I speak.

I'm gonna get some more coffee. You want some?

My Father looks at my Mother. My Mother shakes her head no and her expression tells me she's still hurt. My Father looks back at me.

I think we're fine.

I stand and I walk back to the coffee machine. As I fill my cup, a tall and thin man dressed like my Father rings a bell hanging near the door. Everyone turns toward him. He tells us that we're going to split into groups and that the groups will meet in separate Rooms. He points to a pair of doors against the wall opposite the glass wall and he starts reading names. When People hear their names called, they stand and they go through the doors. As I walk back to the corner where my Parents are sitting, the man says my name. I continue toward my Parents and when I reach them, I speak.

Looks like I've got to go.

My Father nods, my Mother looks like she's going to cry. I turn and I start to walk away. My Father speaks.

James?

I turn around.

We're sorry about the smoking remarks.

My Mother nods. Tears start running down her cheeks.

We know you've got a lot that you're trying to deal with right now and we know you're doing the best you can, so if you need to, it's okay if you smoke around us.

I smile. This simple gesture breaks my heart.

Thank you.

My Father smiles, and beneath her tears, my Mother smiles. Her smile makes me feel a little better.

I'll see you tonight.

I turn and I walk to my door. I walk through it and I enter another large Room. It is white, bright and cheery. There are inspirational pictures on the walls with phrases like Take It Day by Day, Let Go and Let God, Easy Does It. There is thick carpet on the floor and there are folding chairs spread in a wide circle around the Room. There are People sitting in the chairs. I find an empty chair without anybody on either side of it and I sit down. I am alone for a moment, but then a pregnant woman sits on one side of me and a gray-haired man sits on the other. The Room fills up, and for every Patient here there are about three Family Members. Everyone looks nervous.

A woman walks in she's in her thirties wearing khakis and Birkenstocks and wool socks and a chorded sweater. She has brown hair, green eyes and looks as if she could be a model. She sits in the only empty chair in the circle and she smiles.

Welcome to your first Group Session at the Family Program.

There are nods, a couple People say thank you.

What we're going to do in this session is introduce ourselves and ask each other questions. Family Members often ask those of us in recovery about what we do or why we do what we do or what it feels like to do it, those of us in recovery often ask Family Members how our actions affect them or how they feel when they're dealing with us or why they deal with us in the ways they do or why they deal with us at all. You should feel free to ask whatever you want, as long as it's not intended to hurt someone's feelings. I'll start with the introductions.

She smiles.

My name is Sophie, and I'm an Addict and an Alcoholic.

Everyone says Hello, Sophie. The man sitting next to her smiles, speaks.

I'm Tony, and I'm the Husband of an Alcoholic.

Everyone says Hello, Tony, and the introductions move around the Room. Mother of a Heroin Addict, Meth Addict, Wife of a Crack Addict, Alcoholic, Son and Daughter of an Alcoholic, Vicodin Addict, Pregnant Wife of a Crack Addict. There are all types of relations, all types of Addicts and Alcoholics. After the introductions, the questions are supposed to start. At first, no one speaks. People stare at the floor, stare at their hands, stare at each other. There are awkward smiles and frustrated sighs. After a few moments, a man who identified himself as a Meth Addict asks how long this session is going to last. Everyone laughs. A woman who identified herself as the Wife of an Alcoholic asks the same thing. How long does this last? Sophie smiles and asks her if she's referring to addiction. The woman nods and says yes. Sophie says addiction lasts a lifetime. It lasts a lifetime.

From there the questions start to flow. How does it feel to be Addicted to something. Horrible. Why does it feel that way. Because we know what we're doing to ourselves and what we're doing to you and we can't stop doing it. What does it feel like when you want it. Need, overwhelming need, uncontrollable need, unimaginable need. What does it feel like when you get it. Relief, followed by horror, followed by more need. Why can't you stop. I don't know. Why can't you stop. I don't know. Why can't you stop. I don't know.

There are other simpler, more technical questions. What is crack and how do you use it. Crack is cocaine cooked with ethyl alcohol, gas and baking powder. We smoke it with a pipe. Where do you buy heroin and how much does it cost. You buy heroin from a dealer and it is very expensive. What is meth and how is it made. Meth is speed and it is made by cooking asthma medicine called ephedrine, formaldehyde, sometimes gas or fertilizer, and baking powder. What does it do to you. Robs you of your heart, robs you of your soul, takes away the ability and the desire to eat and to sleep, robs you of your sanity.

The Addicts and Alcoholics give straight, simple answers. We ask no questions. Unlike the Family Members, we already know the answers. We fuck up your lives. We ruin every single one of your days. We are your worst nightmare. You don't know what to do with us. You're at the end of your rope. You don't know what to do. You're at the end of your fucking rope. You don't know what to do. At the end of the Session, Sophie asks everyone to join hands. An intimacy has developed and we do so eagerly. She has us recite a poem that she calls the Serenity Prayer. She says a line and we follow. God grant me the serenity to accept the things I cannot change, the courage to change the things I can, and the wisdom to know the difference. She smiles we smile everyone smiles. When we finish saying the prayer, she has us do it again. God grant me the serenity to accept the things I cannot change, the courage to change the things I can, and the wisdom to know the difference. She has us do it again and again.

When she stands, everyone else stands. She tells us we're finished and everyone starts hugging each other. There are hugs sealing the bonds hugs healing the wounds hugs in appreciation of knowledge and insight shared hugs of under-standing and hugs of compassion extended. After the hugs, Sophie opens the door and we file out smiling and laughing and in better shape then when we en-tered. Everyone says good-bye thank you good-bye thank you.

The Primary Patients walk through the Halls to the Dining Hall. We do so as a group. The men talk to the men, the women talk to the women. It is all small talk, meaningless bullshit like where you from, how long you been here, what's your drug of choice. The talk continues as we walk through the Glass Corridor and we form a line. It continues as we get trays and food.

The talk stops when it's time to decide where to sit. Nearly everyone seeks out an empty table. The rest of the Patients have yet to arrive, so there are plenty from which to choose. I find a table where no one is anywhere near me and I sit down. I eat slowly. I stare at my plate, move my fork toward it, scoop, move the fork toward my mouth. I chew. I don't pay attention to what I'm chewing, and after a few bites, it doesn't matter. Everything tastes the same. Fork to plate, fork to mouth. Chew. Everything tastes the same.

My plate is empty. The rest of the Patients are arriving and the Dining Hall is starting to fill up. I stand with my tray and I put it on the conveyor and I walk out. I go back to the Unit and I go to my Room. I have some time to burn be-fore I am meeting my Parents. I should be prepared. As calm as I can be in order to control the Fury, which I know will come. Lilly makes me calm, but Lilly is not here. Free air makes me calm. The little book the Tao makes me calm and it is sitting near my bed. I sit down on my bed and I open the book at random and I start to read.

Fifteen. Be as careful as crossing frozen water, alert as a Warrior on enemy ground. Be as courteous as a Guest, as fluid as a Stream. Be as shapeable as a block of wood, as receptive as a glass. Don't seek and don't expect. Be patient and wait until your mud settles and your water is clear. Be patient and wait. Your mud will settle. Your water will be clear.

Sixty-three. Act without doing, work without effort, think of the large as small and the many as few. Confront the difficult while it is easy, accomplish the great one step at a time. Don't reach and you will find, if you run into trouble throw yourself toward it. Don't cling to comfort and everything will be comfortable.

Seventy-nine. Failure is an opportunity. If you blame others, there is no end to blame. Fulfill your obligations, correct your mistakes. Do what you need to do and step away. Demand nothing and give all. Demand nothing and give all.

Twenty-four. Stand on your toes and you won't stand firm. Rush ahead and you won't go far. Try to shine and you'll extinguish your light. Try to define yourself, you won't know who you are. Don't try to control others. Let go and let them be.

As I read this book it calms me without effort, fills in the blanks of my strategy for survival. Control by letting go of control, fix your problems by forgetting they're problems. Deal with them and the World and yourself with patience and simplicity and compassion. Let things be, let yourself be, let everything be and accept it as it is. Nothing more. Nothing less. Nothing more.

I am prepared. I am calm. I will accept what comes. I walk out of the Room. My Parents are waiting for me on the other side of the Clinic.

I walk through the Halls. My eyes are forward but focused on nothing. Each step is a step and nothing more than a step, a method for taking me from this place to that place. As I turn corners I hear sounds. They sound as they are, they just sound as they sound. The Tao told me what I needed to hear and I listened. The Tao taught me what I needed to be taught and I learned. The sounds just sound.

I stop in front of the door to Joanne's Office. I knock on it. Her voice says come in so I open the door and I go inside. My Mother and my Father are sitting on the couch. They have changed clothes again and they are holding hands. Their eyes are dry and their lips steady. They stand to greet me, but they don't try to hug me. I say hello to them and I don't try to hug them either. I sit down in the chair across from them and they sit back down. Joanne is behind her desk. She's smoking a cigarette.

Your Parents told me about their new smoking policy and they extended it to me. I hope you don't mind.

I pull out a cigarette.

Not at all.

I reach for an ashtray.

We were talking about our Session this morning. Your Parents have some thoughts and feelings on it, but we thought we'd start with yours.

I light my cigarette, take a drag. I exhale.

I hated this morning.

Joanne looks at me.

I think you need to be more specific and I think you need to tell your Parents, not me.

I look at my Parents. They are holding hands and they are looking at me.

I'm sorry about what I told you this morning. It must have been terrible for you to have to sit through it. As I was doing it, I felt a number of things. The first was anger. Intense anger. I don't know why, but whenever I'm near you, I feel incredibly and uncontrollably angry. The second feeling I had was horror. Horror because as I get some distance from myself, I'm realizing what a truly horrible Person I am. I've hidden a lot from you, as much as I could, and I can't imagine what it must have been like for you to have to sit through the details of my monstrous existence.

I take another drag of my smoke. My Mother moves closer to my Father, my Father holds her a little tighter.

I felt shame, enormous amounts of shame. I felt shame because of who I am,

I step forward, put one of my arms around each of them, and they each put one of their arms around me. We pull each of us pulls and we hug each other the three of us hug each other it is strong and easy and full of something maybe love. The Fury flares and I am momentarily uncomfortable, but the strength I am giving and the strength I am taking kills it. Easily and quickly. The giving and taking kills it.

We separate. My Parents are still smiling. I say good-bye to Joanne and she says good-bye to me. I open the door and I wait. My Parents say good-bye and thank you to Joanne and she smiles and says no problem. They walk out and I follow them. We say good-bye outside the door and they go one way and I go another.

I walk back to the Unit. I know my way the walk is automatic. I am tired and I'm ready for bed. I don't want to deal with anything or anybody. I don't want to think about Prison or genetics or ear infections. I don't know about one and the other two don't matter. I want to sleep. Close my eyes and sleep.

I get to my Room open the door walk inside. Miles is in bed he is already sleeping. The light on my nightstand is on I turn it off get under the covers. They are warm. The pillow is soft.

I am tired.

I go to sleep.

There are hands shaking me gently shaking me. I hear my name James James James I am being shaken. I hear my name. James.

I open my eyes. It is dark I can see the blurred shape shaking me and saying my name. I blink once. Twice. It is dark. I can see.

Miles is standing above me. He sees my eyes I see his eyes. He lets me go. I sit up.

There's a young lady at the window for you.

What?

A young lady is at the window. She's asking for you.

I lean forward, look around him. I see an outline through the glass.

Fuck.

Miles laughs.

Women are difficult. They become more so if you ignore them. I'd suggest you go speak to her.

Fuck.

I push away the covers, Miles steps back. I drag myself from my bed and I walk to the window and I open it. A rush of cold of a cold wind slaps me in the face. I stick my head out the window. Lilly is standing in the shadows. She speaks.

I need to talk to you.

Right now?

Yes.

Can't wait till morning?

I need to talk to you.

Hold on.

I step away from the window and I close it. I turn around and Miles is smiling at me.

You knew it couldn't wait till morning if she woke us up in the middle of the night.

I thought I'd try.

I put on my pants.

There's no use trying with them. You just do.

My shoes.

That'll be my Policy in the future.

Hank's jacket.

It's the best way.

I walk back to the window.

Sorry you got woken up.

Miles smiles.

Don't get caught.

I smile.

I won't.

I open the window, get hit by the cold the cold the cold. I climb through and I close the window behind me. Lilly is in the shadows. I walk toward her.

Hi.

That's all you've got to say?

What's that supposed to mean?

You think you can say hi to me and everything will be cool?

What are you talking about?

I stop walking and I stand in front of her. I can see swollen eyes and the stains of tears. I see her rear and swing. One step back and she misses.

What the fuck is your problem?

She regains her balance and she steps forward and she pushes me.

Fuck you.

I laugh. She pushes me again.

You think this is funny?

She pushes me again.

Fuck you.

Her voice is getting louder. She pushes again.

Fuck you.

She rears back.

FUCK YOU.

She swings. I grab her arm. She swings with the other. I grab that one. She struggles and she clenches her teeth and I hold her arms and I drag her away from the Building, trying to be gentle, but using enough strength to move her. She says let me go let me go you fucking Asshole let me go. I ignore her. I walk slowly back-ward, holding her arms and gently pulling her into the darkness.

Fifty feet away we're safe. I keep pulling, she keeps struggling and swearing and calling me names. A hundred feet away we're safer. The darkness is darker. The sound carries less. I stop walking and pulling, but I don't let go. She struggles. I put my arms around her and I hold her tight.

Calm down.

No.

I'm not letting go of you.

I'll make you.

She struggles more. I hold tighter. Her body is against mine, her arms are pressed against the flesh of each chest. I hold her and she struggles. I wait and she swears. When she stops after a few moments she stops I hold her still. She breathes. Deep heavy breaths. In the silence of night. In the darkness where we're safe.

Her breathing slows slows slows. I lay my head on her shoulder. When she is breathing normally I speak.

You all right?

No.

What's wrong?

You're an Asshole.

Why am I an Asshole?

You talked to him. Why didn't you show up?

When?

You talked to that Motherfucker on your Unit.

I don't know what you're talking about.

Where were you today?

When?

At three o'clock.

In a session at the Family Center.

You were supposed to be with me.

I didn't know that.

You had three plates at lunch. Three o'clock.

I didn't know we were doing that today.

Why'd you think I was staring at you during dinner?

I had no idea. I thought you looked upset, but I didn't know why.

Why didn't you call me?

You always call me.

So what?

I don't have the number.

That's bullshit.

No, it's not.

That's an excuse. You should have called me.

Give me the number and next time I will.

She pushes herself away me from slightly away but she keeps her arms around me. She looks down at the ground and at the blackness near her feet. She looks up. Clear water blue into pale green. She smiles, barely smiles, not a happy smile but a smile of regret. Of sadness. A smile of mistake and of misunderstanding. She speaks.

I'm sorry.

Why?

I got scared.

Why were you scared?

I was scared you were leaving me.

I'm not going to do that.

I was scared after I told you those things about me that you didn't want to see me anymore. Then I thought somebody on your Unit told you something else.

Those things don't bother me. Nothing I hear is going to bother me.

I thought they did, and when you didn't show up, I thought I knew for sure.

The only thing you need to know for sure is that I'm not leaving.

She smiles. This time it's a real smile.

Ever?

Yes. Ever.

You're sure?

I am.

I don't want to be alone anymore, James.

You won't be.

I cried all day.

Don't cry again. Just think of the word ever.

She smiles brighter, wider, a smile more full of what she is, which is beautiful. Inside and out. The smile. Her. Beautiful. She leans forward and she steps to her toes and she closes her eyes and she kisses me. Long and sweet and slow. I could keep kissing her forever.

We separate. I tell her we should go. Not back, but farther into the darkness. We start walking, hand in hand, slow steps, there's no hurry. The Woods are alive at night. Twigs cracking, leaves rustling, branches swaying. Moon sitting, clouds drifting. Shadows dancing and threatening and disappearing. Small animals fighting and chattering and foraging for food. Small animals hiding. The living Wood.

As we walk we talk. Lilly needs to talk about her feelings about her worries about her fears. I let her. I encourage her. I listen to her. Though the stains of tears have been wiped away from the softness of her cheek, the cause of her tears remains alive and full not faded not yet. She talks softly and easily and without hesitation. She talks of her feelings of being left in the past. By her Father and by the Boy in Chicago and by everyone she has ever cared about in her entire life. They left her and they never called and they never sent a letter, never showed her that they loved her, never came back. Not once. Not ever.

She talks about the desertion. How each time it broke her heart. How with each break it became harder to heal. How with each time she healed, it became harder to love again. How each time hope faded into desolation. Into loneliness and despair. Into self-hatred and self-loathing. At the beginning there was hope. It faded. At the end there was nothing.

She talks about me in relation to her life. She is seeking freedom. That is all she wants, all she desires, all she hopes to achieve. Freedom. Not just from chemicals but from the cycle of loving and losing, risking and failing, returning to that which she abhors each time returning. She thought she had lost me ear-

I walk out of the Bathroom. Miles is sitting on the edge of his bed waiting
for me.
Are you going to Dinner?
I'm supposed to stay here.
For how long?
I don't know.
Would you like me to get you something to eat?
Sure.
What would you like?
Whatever's easy.
Okay.
Thank you.
Anything I can help you with?
You know what time it is?
He looks at his watch.
Six-fifteen.
Thank you.
I walk to my bed. He stands and he walks to the door.
If you're not here when I get back, I'll leave whatever I bring you on your
nightstand.
Thanks, Miles.
He walks out, closes the door behind him. I lie down on my bed I am cold I
start to shake I climb under the covers. I curl into myself and I close my eyes
and I bury my face into my chest and into the bed. I fall into a sleep where I
am not asleep. A state of heavy consciousness neither aware nor unaware. My
body relaxes my body shuts down my body rests. My mind slows, holds im-
ages, wishes, mistakes, reality. They are like thick surreal photographs. I look at
them in my mind and they sit there. I am sleeping but not I'm not asleep. I am
aware and unaware.
The door opens again I open my eyes. I lift my head and I see Lincoln standing
under the door frame. There is light behind him he speaks.
Time to get up.
Okay.
Come to my Office when you're ready.
Okay.
He turns and he leaves and he closes the door as he goes. I get out of bed and I
walk to the Bathroom and I turn on the water and I splash some of the water
over my face. It runs down my cheeks and over my lips and into my mouth
and it tastes good. I lean over and I take a sip. Another another another.
Straight from the faucet. It's good.
I leave my Room and walk through the silent Hall. The Unit is empty, the
men at Dinner. I go to the coffee machine and I get a cup and I take a sip and
it immediately wakes me.

As I walk down the stairs, I start to get nervous. The coffee burns my stomach and I can feel my blood moving through my veins. My legs are unsteady, and I think about each step. In front of the other. In front of the other.

I cross the Lower Level walk into the short Hall leading to Lincoln's Office. The Hall is dark, though there is light at the end where his door is open. I think about each step. As I enter his Office, I have to think about each step. He is sitting behind his desk.

Shut the door.

I turn and I shut the door. I turn back and he motions to a chair across from him. I sit and he leans back in his chair and he stares at me. I stare back.

If it were up to me you'd be gone. I don't like your attitude, and I don't think you've made much of an effort, and I think your continued resistance to what we try to do here, which is help People, has been detrimental to both the Unit and to yourself.

He stares. I stare back.

That being said, you're being given another chance. If you behave and work hard and follow the Rules, you will be able to stay until your Program runs its course. If you violate any of the Rules, even something as simple as not doing your morning Job or saying anything more than hello to any woman not on our Staff, you will be asked to leave. You think you can do that?

I smile. I'm relieved.

Yes, I can. Thank you.

Don't thank me, I wanted you out. Thank Joanne. Just like before, she's the one who saved you.

Thanks anyway.

You can go now.

He looks down at some papers on his desk. I wait. When he looks up, I speak.

Is Lilly staying?

No, she's not.

My relief disappears.

You kicked her out?

Panic returns.

When we told her she wouldn't be allowed to see you anymore, she walked out.

You didn't stop her?

When people want to leave, we let them leave. Our Job is to help people who want to stay and be helped.

What if I told you I knew where she was going?

Doesn't matter.

I know where she's going. I could get her and bring her back.

He chuckles, and instantly the panic is gone. The Fury rises.

Why's that funny?

We discourage relationships because they generally turn out this way. People think they can solve each other's problems, and it's just not the case. I hope this will teach you a lesson.

What's that supposed to mean?

We know what we're doing here. We have Rules for a reason. Maybe you'll listen a bit better from now on.

Fuck you.

What did you say?

She's a Person, not a fucking lesson.

What did you just say to me?

I said fuck you, you fucking Asshole. She's not a fucking lesson.

One more remark like that and you're out of here.

You think I want to stay here now?

If you want to stay sober you will.

I'm not gonna stay in a place where Assholes like you say that their Job is to help People, but when someone needs help most, you deny it to them because they believe in something different than you or need a different kind of help than what you think is right.

Do what you need to do.

I will, and I'm gonna stay clean doing it, if for no other reason than to be able to come back here and show your self-righteous ass that your way isn't the only way.

Good luck.

Fuck you.

I stand and I leave. I walk through the Unit and I go to my Room. I grab the little book the *Tao* put on my warmest clothes a sweater two pairs of socks another pair of socks over my hands. It's cold I can see it through the window. I leave my Room good-bye good-bye good-bye. I walk through the Halls I will never have to see these fucking Halls again fuck you good-bye. I walk through the Reception Area hit the front door I am out of the Clinic. Fuck you and good-bye. I am out.

I start walking. It's cold and dark, there's no light and no Moon. I follow the road the one road in the one road out. I see the outlines of trees and the mist of my breath. I hear rocks and gravel crush beneath my feet.

I don't remember coming in, it was so long ago, but I know this road ends on a larger road. There will be cars on the larger road. I will try to get a ride. Locals will know where I'm from and they won't pick me up, but Trucks might pick me up or people passing through on their way somewhere else might pick me up. My face is healed. I don't look like the image of an Alcoholic and a drug Addict and a Criminal anymore. I look normal though I'm not. A Truck might pick me up or someone passing through might pick me up. The locals won't get near me. They will know what I am.

I smile again.

Three to six months in County Jail. I have to report within ten days.

Leonard smiles, Miles speaks.

Are you happy with that?

I nod.

Yeah, I'm very happy.

Miles nods.

Good.

I think you two had something to do with it, so I want to say thank you.

Leonard looks at Miles, Miles looks at Leonard. Leonard speaks.

Did you do something?

Miles shakes his head.

No. Did you?

Leonard shakes his head.

No, I didn't do anything.

Miles smiles.

And if you had, considering our positions on the opposite ends of the legal spectrum, you certainly wouldn't have discussed it with me.

Leonard smiles.

No fucking way. I get nervous discussing the weather with you.

Miles laughs. I speak.

Is that how we're playing this?

They both look at me. They are both smiling. Miles speaks.

Consider yourself a very fortunate young man, James.

Leonard nods.

Very fucking fortunate.

I smile.

Thank you.

Miles stands and says he needs to make some phone calls, Leonard stands and says he has some business to take care of before tonight. I walk up the stairs and I go to my Room and I open the door and I sit down on my bed and I pick up my book. I have missed it my little Chinese book.

Forty-four. What is more important, fame or integrity. What is more valuable, money or happiness. What is more dangerous, success or failure. If you look to others for fulfillment, you will never be fulfilled. If your happiness depends on money, you will never be happy. Be content with what you have and take joy in the way things are. When you realize you have all you need, the World belongs to you.

Thirty-six. If you want to shrink something, you must first expand it. If you want to get rid of something, you must first allow it to flourish. If you want to take something, you must allow it to be given. The soft will overcome the hard. The slow will beat the fast. Don't tell people the way, just show them the results.

Seventy-four. If you understand that all things change constantly change, there is nothing you will hold on to, all things change. If you aren't afraid of dying, there is nothing you can't do. Trying to control the future is like trying to take the place of the Master Carpenter. When you handle the Master Carpenter's tools, chances are that you'll cut your hand.

Thirty-three. Knowing other people is intelligence, knowing yourself is wisdom. Mastering other people is strength, mastering yourself is power. If you realize that what you have is enough, you are rich truly rich. Stay in the center and embrace peace, simplicity, patience and compassion. Embrace the possibility of death and you will endure. Embrace the possibility of life and you will endure.

This little book feeds me. It feeds me food I didn't know existed, feeds me food I wanted to taste, and have never tasted before, food that will nourish me and keep me full and keep me alive. I read it and it feeds me. It lets me see what my life is in simple terms, it simply is what it is, and I can deal with my life on those terms. It is not complicated unless I make it so. It is not difficult unless I allow it to be. A second is no more than a second, a minute no more than a minute, a day no more than a day. They pass. All things and all time will pass. Don't force or fear, don't control or lose control. Don't fight and don't stop fighting. Embrace and endure. If you embrace, you will endure.

I set down the book and I close my eyes. I don't feel peace and I don't feel chaos. I don't have hope nor do I lack it. I am not anxious and I am not in a hurry. What I feel isn't time slipping away it is simply time passing as it does and as it should pass. What is going to happen is going to happen. It is simply life and the events that occur during the term of life. Just as I am accepting that I am on my bed right now in this moment unmoving and still my eyes closed and my body quiet, I will accept the events of my life as they come. I will deal with them. Good and bad they will both come. I will accept them in the way that I am accepting myself right now. Let them come.

I open my eyes and I pick up the book and I read more. I read words like harmony, contentment, humility, understanding, intuition, nourishment. I read words like open, fluid, receptive, balanced, core. I read that if you close your mind in judgments and traffic in desire your heart will be troubled. I read that if you keep your mind from judging and aren't led by the senses your heart will find peace. I read close your mouth, block your senses, blunt your sharpness. I read untie your knots soften your glare settle your dust. I read that if you want to know the World, look inside your heart. I read that if you want to know yourself, look inside your heart. I set the book down I set it against my chest. I close my eyes my bed feels warm and soft against my back. I don't move I just lie there warm and soft against my back. Quietly breathing.

Thinking.

Not thinking.

Of me.

Of the World.

As it is.

The bed is soft and warm against my back.

I lie there.

The door opens I hear it. It has been a while I don't know how long. I hear the door and I open my eyes and Miles comes in his eyes are swollen. I sit up.

What's going on?

He walks to his bed, sits down.

I've been on the phone with my Wife for the last hour and a half.

How'd it go?

He looks down and he shakes his head. I stand up and I walk over to him and I lean over and I put my arms around him and I hug him. He hugs me back and he starts crying. I don't know what to say, so I say nothing. I hug him and I let him hug me and I hope that somehow and in whatever way, I am helping him. I don't know what his Wife said, but I know he needs help. His crying becomes sobbing becomes violent sobbing. He squeezes me tight. I have my arms around him they are my only weapon against his grief. We sit and he cries and I hold him. Whatever has happened has happened he'll talk about it if he wants to talk my arms are my only weapon. We sit and Miles cries.

Violent sobs become sobs becomes crying. He stops. The Room is silent. It is getting dark the Sun is down the last streaks of fading light slip through our window. He pulls away and he asks me if he can be alone. I stand and I leave the Room. I close the door behind me.

I walk into the Unit, and it is a madhouse. There is a man in a blue jumpsuit installing a cable box on top of the television. There are other men dressed in white pants and white shirts and white shoes setting up banquet tables. Most of the men of the Unit are standing in small groups talking about what's going on and why these people are here. I hear one of the men ask the Cableman why he is here and the Cableman says I am not at liberty to discuss it. I hear another ask one of the Caterers and the Caterer says I am not at liberty to discuss it.

I get a cup of coffee light a cigarette look for somewhere to sit down. I want to sit down alone. As I start to look for an empty chair, a man steps from the Phone Booth and calls my name. I say what and he tells me I have a phone call. I ask him who it is and he says he doesn't know.

I walk to the phone step into the Booth pick up the receiver.

Hello.

Hi, James.

My Mother and Father both say hello. The connection is distant. There is a slight echo and a slight delay.

Hi.

My Mother speaks.

We wanted to apologize, James.

For what?

For having to leave early. We feel terrible about it.

Don't.

Are you sure?

Yeah. I appreciated you coming at all.

My Father speaks.

Thank you, James.

Sure.

Any news?

I heard from Randall.

My Mother speaks.

What'd he say?

Three to six months in County Jail in Ohio. Three years probation. If I stay out of trouble, my Record gets cleared.

My Father speaks.

That's great news. How'd it happen?

I chuckle.

I'm not sure.

My Mother speaks.

Why are you laughing?

I'm just happy. This is a big load off my shoulders.

My Father speaks.

When do you go?

Sometime in the next ten days.

When are you leaving there?

I don't know, but soon.

There is silence. I can feel my Parents thinking about me, their youngest Son, sitting in a Jail cell. The silence is dense, and it is punctuated by deep breaths and footsteps. I hear my Mother start to cry and the echo doubles, my Father is standing with her. He asks if he can call me back and I tell him yes and he tells me he loves me and I tell him I love him and we hang up.

I open the door of the Phone Booth and I step back into the Unit. The banquet tables have been set up and they are covered with white tableclothes, white plates, forks and knives and glasses. I don't see the Caterers, but I know they are nearby because of the smell, which is of rich, strong, hot food. The smell makes me instantly hungry instantly ravenous. I want it right now. Ten heaping plates of it right fucking now.

I walk up to the Upper Level. I stand with Matty and Ted. I ask them if they know what's going on. Matty says no, but he's hungry and if he don't get some gosh darn food soon he's going to go fricking crazy. Ted just shrugs and says he has no idea.

Lincoln walks into the Unit, looks around and speaks.

Everyone here?

The men look at each other. A voice I don't know replies.

Miles isn't here.

Another Voice.

And Leonard isn't here.

Lincoln speaks.

Anyone know where Miles is?

I speak.

In our Room. I don't think he wants to be disturbed.

He nods, speaks.

Anyone seen Leonard?

The men look at each other.

Anyone?

They shake their heads.

Anyone?

Lincoln smiles, raises his voice.

Leonard.

He does it again, but louder.

Leonard.

He yells.

LEONARD.

Down one of the Halls, music starts playing. It is the theme song from a famous boxing movie about an unknown Palooka from Philadelphia who almost wins the Heavyweight Championship. All of the men smile, a few laugh. The music comes closer, gets louder, and everyone turns toward a doorway through which Leonard, in a bright white suit, comes bursting out. He has a small boom box in one of his hands, the other is raised in a fist above his head.

There is cheering, laughing, a few men throw candy wrappers or pieces of paper at him. He stands next to Lincoln, turns off the boom box, motions for silence. When it comes, he speaks.

We have cause for celebration, my friends.

There is more cheering. Leonard waits for it to stop and he speaks again.

Early yesterday, I was told by our friend Lincoln that tomorrow, I will be set free. In honor of that, and in honor of all of you, and in honor of this place, tonight we feast.

More cheering. Leonard and Lincoln smile. When the cheering stops, Leonard speaks.

I've had steaks and lobsters brought in from Minneapolis, we'll have apple pie and ice cream for dessert, and in between, we will watch the World Heavyweight Championship.

The men go wild, cheering and yelling and clapping. They start rushing down to thank Leonard and Lincoln and shake their hands. As they do, the sliding-

Hall and I eat dinner with Miles and Michael. After dinner I go to the Lecture, but I don't listen to it. After the Lecture, I go back to my Room.
I try to read, but I can't.
I climb into bed and I try to sleep.
There is one thing.
That haunts me.
Still.

sleep through the night. Without interruption, without the aid of chemicals. It is the second night in a row I have slept without interruption and without drugs and alcohol. It is a new record.

When I wake it is morning early morning. Not dark, but not yet light. It is gray. Gray like fading sadness, gray like rising fear. Not dark, but not yet light.

I get out of bed. Miles is asleep I walk quietly to the Bathroom. I shower and I shave and I brush my teeth. I get dressed and I leave the Room.

I get a cup of coffee and I sit down at a table and I drink the coffee and I smoke cigarettes and I watch the men do their morning Jobs. One cleans the kitchen, one takes out the garbage, one vacuums the floor. I see a man carrying the supplies for the Group Toilets. They seem so long ago. The Group Toilets. Roy. So long ago.

I finish the coffee. I walk through the Halls to the Dining Hall. I get another cup of coffee and I look for a table. Matty is alone in the corner I sit with him.

He stares at his food. I can see his eyes they are bloodshot and swollen.

A fork shakes in his hand. A glass shakes in the other. He stares at his food. I speak.

You okay, Matty?

He shakes his head.

What's wrong?

He shakes his head.

Is there anything I can do?

He shakes his head.

Do you want me to leave?

He shakes his head.

I sit with him. I sit with him and I sip my coffee. He sits and he stares at his food. His hands shake and he doesn't speak. He just stares at his food. I finish my coffee and I stand and I ask him if he needs anything. He looks up at me and he speaks.

Don't leave.

I sit back down.

Okay.

He looks at me. His eyes are bloodshot and swollen.

I need someone to sit with me.

I'm here.

He looks at me. His eyes are bloodshot and swollen.

It's over, James.

What do you mean?

My fucking life. It's fucking done.

What are you talking about?

He sets down his fork, releases his glass. His hands continue to shake.

I found out my Wife started smoking.

Started smoking what?

He starts to break down.

The fucking rock.

He stops himself.

Shit, Matty. I'm sorry.

He shakes his head.

She had never done it before. She was supposed to take care of our Kids until I got out of here. She got all fucking curious about what the shit was and why it did what it did to me and she went out and she fucking tried some.

How'd you find out?

My Grandma called me. Said she went by the house and found the Kids alone. They hadn't been fed in a couple of days and our little one was sitting on the floor in a dirty fucking diaper. She waited there till my Wife came back and when she did, she was all fucked up and babbling and shit and she said she'd been out smoking.

I'm sorry, Matty.

Ain't your fucking fault.

What are you gonna do?

I don't fucking know. My fucking Wife has always been the one that held us together while I was out fucking up, and if she's on the shit, things are gonna fall the fuck apart. You can't have Kids or have a Family with two Parents that are Rockheads, and I probably won't be able to stay clean if she's fucking smoking.

What about getting her some help and going back to boxing?

Look at me, James, I can't fucking fight no more. My body is wrecked, my head is all fucked up. I wouldn't last thirty fucking seconds in a Ring with the worst fucking fighters in the World. And as much as I want her to get help, we spent the last chunk of my fighting money paying for me to come here and we ain't got nothing else. We ain't got fucking shit.

Can I do anything to help?

Not unless you got a big-ass chunk of money sitting around that you want to give me.

I don't.

I'm fucked, James. It's all over.

Something will work out.

I seen too much of the fucking rock to believe that bullshit. I'm gonna die, she's gonna die, and our Kids gonna grow up to be just like us. We're all fucked. Totally fucked.

He stands.

I gotta go for a fucking walk.

He picks up his tray.

Thanks for listening to me.

He walks away. I watch him. I pick up my coffee cup and I stand and I walk to the conveyor and I set my cup on it. I walk down the Glass Corridor separating men and women. I see Miles and Ted walking toward me. They are close together and their heads are turned down. Their lips are moving, but barely. Miles looks up at me and he gives me a slight nod acknowledging me and he continues speaking to Ted. They walk past me. I leave them alone.

I go back to my Room. I open the nightstand next to my bed. I take the stack of paper the twenty-two pages and I put them in the pocket of my pants. I leave my Room and I walk through the Halls. They are gray like the morning like fading sadness like rising fear. I am aware of them, but they don't bother me. I know them too well. They don't bother me.

I knock on Joanne's door she says come in. I open the door and I step inside. She is sitting behind her desk, reading the paper, drinking coffee, smoking a cigarette. She speaks.

How are you?

I'm good.

You ready?

Yeah, I'm ready.

Anything you want to talk about before we go?

No.

She sets down her paper, stubs out her cigarette.

After lunch today, I need you to come back here. Ken and I want to go over some things with you.

Is everything okay?

We have a Recovery Plan we'd like you to follow after you leave here.

Anything in it I'll actually do?

Probably not, but it would be irresponsible not to present it to you.

Okay.

You want to go?

Yeah.

She stands. We walk out of her Office and through the Halls. The Halls are still gray, though a few shades darker, like deeper sadness, like greater fear. We do not talk as we walk, and with each step, the memory of that night grows stronger. I just wanted to be alone. I was crying. He came to me and I destroyed him. His spilling blood. I fucking destroyed him.

We stop at a door. A sign on the door reads Father David, Chaplain, Religious Services. Joanne knocks on the door a voice says come in. She tells me to wait for a moment and she opens the door and she walks inside and she closes the door behind her.

I stand and I wait. I start to shake my hands and legs and lips are shaking. My heart is shaking. If they were part of me, the Halls would be black. With sadness and fear. With the darkest darkness that lives within me. They would be jet fucking black. I am shaking.

The door opens. Joanne steps out and she stands in front of me. She speaks.

He's ready for you.

All right.

I told him there might be some uncomfortable moments. He said it's probably nothing he hasn't heard before.

We'll see.

Good luck.

Thank you.

She reaches out and she puts her arms around me and she hugs me. She speaks.

You'll feel better when it's over.

I nod. She lets go of me. I reach for the door my arm is heavy. I pull the door it weighs a thousand pounds. I open it and I don't want to go in I don't want to do this. Joanne is standing behind me and I turn and I look at her and she smiles and her smile allows me to step forward. Into the Office. I close the door behind me.

A Priest sits behind a desk. He is wearing black he is wearing a white collar. He is old, in his seventies, he has gray hair and dark brown eyes. A Crucifix hangs on the wall behind him, a worn leather Bible sits on top of a stack of papers. It is the first time since that night that I have been in the presence of a Priest. As I stare at him, the Fury rises. He stands and he looks at me and he speaks.

Hello, my Son. My name is Father David.

All due respect Sir, but I'm not your Son. My name is James.

Hello, James.

Hello.

Would you like to sit down?

He motions to a chair on the far side of his desk. It is across from him. I sit down.

Thank you.

He sits in his chair.

You're here for your Fifth Step.

I don't believe in the Steps. I'm here to make a Confession.

Are you a Catholic?

No.

I can't take a Confession unless you are a Catholic.

Would you like me to leave?

Are you comfortable calling this a conversation?

Yes.

Why don't we do that.

Thank you.

Do you have any questions before you start?

No.

Do you have any concerns?

No.

You should be reassured that whatever you have to say this morning will never leave this room. It is between you and me and God.

I don't believe in God, sir.

Then it will be between you and me.

Thank you.

Would you like to begin?

Yes.

Take as much time as you need.

I take a deep breath. I pull the twenty-two pages of yellow paper out of my pocket and I set them in my lap. I look at them. They contain everything I can remember except for one thing.

I start reading. I read slowly and methodically. I read every word and I recount every incident. Each page seems as if it takes an hour. As I move through them, I feel better and I feel worse. Better because I am finally admitting my sins and I am finally taking some form of responsibility for them. Worse because as I speak of them, I relive them in my mind. Each and every one of them. I relive them in my mind.

When I am done reading I take another deep breath. I look at the pages and I fold them and I put them back in my pocket. The Priest speaks.

Are you finished?

I shake my head.

No.

It looks like you have read all that you have written.

There was one thing I didn't write about.

Would you like to tell me about it?

Yes.

Take as much time as you need.

I look down. I look at my hands they are shaking. I feel my heart it is beating hard it is scared. I am scared. I take another deep breath I take another. Another. I am scared of speaking scared of the memory. I am scared.

I look up. Into the eyes of Father David. They are deep and dark and in them I do not see what I saw that night. In the eyes of this Priest there is only peace and serenity and the security of his belief. Not what I saw that night. I take another breath, one last breath. I exhale. I speak.

Eighteen months ago in Paris, I beat a man so badly that he may have died. The man was a Priest.

I take another breath.

Right after my arrest in Ohio, while I was sitting in Jail, I started thinking about my life. I was twenty-two years old. I had been an Alcoholic and drug Addict for a decade. I hated myself. I didn't see a future and the only thing in my past was wreckage and disaster. I decided that I wanted to die.

When I got out, and jumped Bail, I flew back to Paris. When I got to my Apartment, I drank a bottle of whiskey and wrote a note. All it said was Don't Mourn Me. I left it on top of my bed and I went out and I started walking toward the nearest Bridge. A lot of Parisians kill themselves that way, by throwing themselves into the Seine. You jump, hit the water, and you either die on impact or you drown.

As I was walking, I started crying. Crying because I had wasted my life and made such a mess of it, and crying because I was happy it was finally going to end. I also started getting scared. Scared because killing yourself isn't an easy thing to do, and I knew that when I did it, everything was over. I don't believe there's a Heaven or anything resembling it. Life just ends.

I take a breath.

I saw a Church and I was getting so scared that I was having trouble walking. I figured I could go inside and it would be quiet and empty and I could sit by myself and think. I found an empty pew and I sat down and I just cried. For a long time. I just sat by there by myself and cried.

I take a deep breath. The Fury that faded while I have been speaking starts to rise again.

After a while, a man, dressed like you, approached me and asked me if I was all right. I told him no. He introduced himself as a Father. He told me that he had a lot of experience counseling young People and that if I wanted to talk to him about my troubles we should go back to his Office and talk. I said no, I'd like to be alone. He sat down next to me and said we should go back to his Office. He told me that he was sure he could help me, just come back to my Office, just come back to my Office. I figured it couldn't hurt, so I went.

I take another breath. The Fury has risen. I speak.

His Office was one of a series of Rooms behind the Altar. When we got there, the Father locked the door behind us. I should have known right fucking then, but he was a Priest, and it didn't cross my mind. I sat down on a couch and he sat down next to me and he asked what was wrong and I told him. I told him about my addictions, about the shitty life I had led, about the disaster I had just run from and about my plan to kill myself. The whole time I talked, he sat

. . .

Michael returned to work at the University. Three weeks later he was arrested for Solicitation of Prostitution and Possession of Crack Cocaine. He died from a self-inflicted gunshot wound.

Roy attacked two Children with a baseball bat. He was sentenced to thirty to fifty years in an Institution for the Criminally Insane in Wisconsin.

Warren fell off the back of a fishing boat in Florida while he was drunk. His body has never been recovered.

The Bald Man started drinking eight weeks after he returned home. His Wife threw him out of their house and his whereabouts are unknown.

Bobby was found dead in New Jersey. He had been shot in the back of the head.

John was caught carrying fourteen ounces of cocaine in San Francisco. He is serving a life sentence without the possibility of parole at San Quentin State Penitentiary in California.

Ed was beaten to death in a Bar fight in Detroit.

Ted was captured by Authorities in Mississippi. He is serving a life term without the possibility of parole at Angola State Farm in Louisiana.

Matty was shot and killed outside of a Crackhouse in Minneapolis.

Miles is alive and well and continues to serve as a Judge. He is still married, had a second Child, a Daughter named Ella, and he has never relapsed.

Leonard returned to Las Vegas and retired. He subsequently died from complications due to AIDS. He was sober until he died. He never relapsed.

Lilly committed suicide by hanging in a Halfway House in Chicago. Her Grandmother had passed away two days earlier. She was found the morning James was released from jail, and it is believed that she was sober until she died.

Lincoln still works at the Clinic.

Ken still works at the Clinic.

Hank and Joanne got married. Both still work at the Clinic.

James has never relapsed.

. . .

· · ·

Thank you Mom and Dad for everything, thank you Mom and Dad. Thank you
Brother Bob and Sister-in-Law Laura. Thank you Maya, I love you Dearest Maya.
Thank you Kassie Evashevski. Thank you Sean McDonald. Thank you Nan Talese.
Thank you David Krintzman. Thank you Preacher and Bella my little Friends.
Thank you Stuart Hawkins, Elizabeth Sosnow, Kevin Yorn, Amar Douglas Rao,
Michael Craven, Quinn Yancey, Christian Yancey, Ingrid Sisson, John Von Brachel,
Helen Motley, Jean Joseph Jr., Joshua Dorfman, Colleen Silva, Eben Strousse,
Chris Wardwell. Thank you Theo, Rigo, Jose and the Boys at the Coffee
Shop on the corner. Thank you Phillip Morris. Thank you Andrew Barash and
Keith Bray. Thank you Kirk, Julie, Kevin. Thank you Lilly, Leonard, Miles,
I love you and I thank you.

the Airbus into Boeing's market are symbolic of that European revenge. Today the Japanese are attacking the same task more effectively, which means that today's challenge for American management is greater by far.

Many of the companies locked in this competitive war are fighting essentially defensive actions, responding (sometimes belatedly) to attack and hoping, at best, to preserve their existing market shares. Very few have turned the tables, coming back from defeat to seize leadership from the overseas challengers and become once again the cynosures, the companies that set the pace and the standards in all respects—technology, market penetration, innovativeness, continuous improvement, and all-round management skill.

It can be done, as proved by the story of one American business and its CEO. The setbacks suffered at the hands of Asian competition had been especially humiliating. Morale at all levels had collapsed in the face of the clear evidence that massive spending had been ill directed and that, under fumbling management, the company was unfit to take on fierce competition. A market that had been thought vital was lost completely—just as a great Japanese company, Sony, virtually lost the VCR market it had created.

Like Sony's Akio Morita and his cohorts, the new American management refused to accept its calamitous setbacks as final. First, with full backing from its financiers, the firm invested enormously in world-beating and state-of-the-art technology, the product of intensive and brilliantly successful R&D. Second, the people working the excellent technology were trained to the highest standards: that showed not just in effectiveness but in their restored morale. Third, their managers, highly trained, well qualified, and carefully selected, reached the top only after much full-time education, technical and general.

Equally important was the organizational structure in which these people were now operating. The general manager in charge of the turnaround had full delegated power to run his operation his way. His instructions from above were absolutely clear, and his full-time chairman gave total support. The same writ ran downward: once allotted their role by the boss, the subordinate managers made their own plans and were expected to execute them decisively.

These subordinate managers weren't enthusiastic when the boss proposed a daring strategy to sweep past the competition. The operating managers gave the classic response: "It can't be done." Their belief that the general manager had lost his marbles only encouraged him. Wouldn't the rival management be saying exactly the same thing? That a grand-slam assault, like the Japanese attack on Detroit, could never win?

That preconception exposed not just an Achilles heel but a yawning gap in the market, which the company exploited at merciless speed. The boss had performed one crucial role of the leader: he turned the negative into a positive by insisting that his managers had to achieve the "impossible." They only agreed, though, after the distribution honcho had pledged in writing that everything would be in place for the launch— everything. That, too, is an elementary and elemental management principle: give people the tools if you want them to finish the job.

There's much more to the story, of course. Those running the company are masters and developers of the most modern techniques (including logistics) and are also deeply immersed in the lessons of history (including those of failure—above all, their own). The top managers, and everybody below them, also have an ample supply of three vital elements: information, planning, and communications. They come in that order, because nothing can be effectively planned without efficient information, and neither information nor planning is any use without communication.

But the planners and the information experts aren't disembodied backroom boys in this company; they are an integral part of all its efforts. The distinction between line and staff is meaningless in modern high-tech circumstances. The best staffers are former line managers, and this company draws its staff largely from this group; staffers are often moved right back into the line as well. As the Japanese have demonstrated, line and staff roles must be inseparable and interchangeable in the drive for global markets.

The outcome was success as total as the previous failure. True, the general manager was lucky in his opposition: his chief opponent, a dominant chairman and CEO who delegated nothing and ruled by fear, had recently made a large, rash, and doomed takeover bid—a description that can be applied to too many chief executives in the West. The truth is that this great turnaround depended on utterly logical and powerful courses of action that happen to highlight some contrary patterns in most big U.S. business today. For utter contrast, consider what the new management did:

1. It *invested* to win leadership in the technology of product and process.
2. It gave effective *power* to people with clear responsibility.
3. It *trained* and educated everybody, from top to bottom, all the time.
4. It led a management *collective* that collaborates, cooperates, and consults.
5. It created the *superstructure* of success by assigning the right roles to the right people.
6. It used the fullest possible *information* for the most ambitious possible strategy.
7. It mastered and developed the new *techniques* of hard and soft management.
8. It linked responsibility, status, and rewards to prime *performance*.
9. It acquired the means of achieving the *impossible*.
10. It unified *organic* strengths to win exemplary success.

Any chief executive, any management, any business, can obey these ten fundamental principles or precepts—although my example isn't, in fact, a business. The general manager was a general, Norman Schwarzkopf, and the company was Desert Storm, Inc. What was demonstrated by the organized body of people and machines known as an army can be emulated by the organized body of people and machines known as a business.

The ten sections of this book, each summarized at the end with my key points of advice, set out those demanding but rewarding fundamentals with the illustration of real-life case histories, both good and bad—frequently in the same case. Perfection isn't given to man, certainly not to business, and every success carries within it not only the seeds of its own decay but current examples of corporate rot. That wondrous economic phenomenon, USA, Inc., is no exception. But if I'm right, and corporate setbacks result from negative behavior, the correct, positive response in peaceful, warlike competition is clear, and its successful outcome is certain.

ONE

Investing in Leadership

1

The Right Stuff

Consider this picture of one nation's management. It is gaining ground against global competitors as its firms, larger and smaller, make great advances in productivity, management, quality, and cost control. Forcing their way into new markets abroad, they are seizing market share from other countries. The nation's top companies are actually enlarging their lead over world rivals. Moreover, this competitive supremacy is continuing to mount, because the enormous progress of its businesses in recent years has created further payoffs whose prime benefits are yet to be realized.

Now consider this savage indictment. A nation's manufacturing prowess has been eroded, in old technologies (notably cars) and new (including computers). Lack of effective domestic competition has opened the door to massive import penetration. Several major manufacturers have been taken over by foreign companies—raising the question of whether the country will "increasingly become a branch-office colony" for Japanese and other foreign owners.

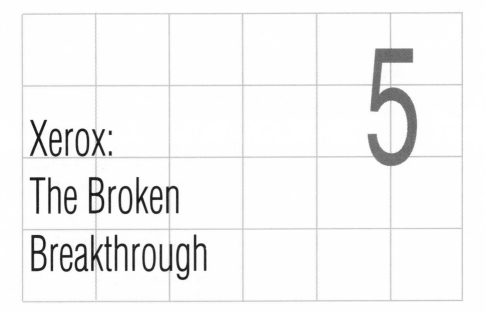

Xerox:
The Broken
Breakthrough

A most extraordinary speech was delivered in 1963 by Peter C. McColough, one of the two prime architects of the Xerox Corporation. Addressing an internal "Talk Leadership Seminar," he asked an arresting question: "Is it inevitable that such organizations as Xerox should have their periods of emergence, full flower of growth and prestige, and then, later, stagnation and death?"

He tracked the development from a "new organization," like the early Xerox, which is "loose on procedure, unclear on organizational lines, variable in policies," to the mature company, which, beset by written and unwritten rules and the "heavy hand of custom," becomes "less venturesome" as it accumulates "possessions, stature, and reputation." That makes it harder to achieve characteristics that every manager would surely want for the organization:

1. It is willing to experiment with a variety of ways to solve its problems.

2. It is flexible and open to the lessons of current experience.
3. It is not bowed by the weight of tradition.

These words (McColough's own) are the very characteristics that writers like Tom Peters (*Thriving on Chaos*) are ramming home as the only way for companies to cope with the shifting complexities of a highly competitive era. But how can they be achieved when McColough's description of the mature business is plainly as accurate in 1992 as in 1963?

1. It develops subtle policies and habitual modes of solving problems.
2. It becomes more efficient, but also less flexible, less willing to look freshly at each day's experience.
3. Its increasingly fixed routines are congealed in an elaborate body of written rules.

As McColough pointed out, "the final stage of organizational senility is that there is a rule or precedent for everything." That sounds terrible enough. But if it's also true (and it must be) that "the written rules are often the least of the problem," what hope is there for the mature company—and the mature manager?

The speech described the *unwritten* rules as "the attitudes and values that accumulate and develop in any organization." Some may actually be "precious assets," like "standards of excellence, loyalty, and high morale." Others constitute a "choking underbrush of custom and precedent. There comes to be an accepted way to do everything. Radical departures from past practices are ruled out. The old hand says, 'You just have to understand how we do things around here,' and what he means is that 'how we do things' is sound and respectable and the best way."

The picture is depressing and familiar. The roots of the disease lie not in the nature of corporate maturity but in that of human beings. Most people like to think of themselves as experiment-minded, flexible, ready to learn from and adapt to what happens day by day, unshackled by tradition. But equally strong human forces encourage all managers to stick to what they know, stand firm by established positions and past experience, and build procedures that keep them from having to think—or rather, to make choices.

One firm way forward in turbulent times is to experiment: to take a limited area of the organization or its product range, and see what happens. What will usually happen is nothing. Experimenting with the new idea (unless it's their own) will carry an implied criticism of the managers—they have perhaps been missing golden opportunities for years. If the experiment succeeds, that will be even worse: their past sins of omission will be explicitly exposed. So one reason why, in McColough's words, young organizations are "flexible and "willing to try anything once" is that their managers have no past record to defend. Their *amour propre* is invested not in the past but in the future—in making a success of this new thing in which they've invested their careers.

Personal investment in the future is what every management needs to discover or recover in the 1990s. Being "willing to try anything once" was the key to the success of McColough and company with xerography. But he wondered out loud to his audience "whether xerography would today pass the test that we now put all new products or ideas through, such as financial analysis, including return on investment, return on sales, technical feasibility, size of market, ability to finance such programs, and so forth."

McColough talked about "our far more sophisticated approach to such problems today and our increasing desire to see things more clearly for the future," and he came to a startling conclusion: "I think there is really a good possibility that we would not have undertaken to do what we actually have done in the xerographic field." There's plenty of evidence to support that stunning statement in what had actually happened.

The inventor of xerography, Chester Carlson, was turned down by, among many others, General Electric, RCA, IBM, and Remington Rand. Only funds from the private Battelle Memorial Institute kept Carlson's "electrophotography" going long enough for Joe Wilson of the small Haloid Company and his chief engineer to see a demonstration—and for Wilson to see at once that here was a miracle in the making. Wilson faced no problems of creativity or communication. But McColough, sitting in Haloid grown large, thought that "one of our greatest obstacles for future growth and vitality is that our people will not feel that they are in the know" and "therefore will become inert and ineffective."

Making a powerful case for creativity, "trying new things and risking failure" and making "inevitable mistakes," McColough delivered a grave warning: "The only stability possible today is stability in motion." And that, remember, was delivered in the much slower-moving world of 1963. It is far truer, and more urgent, today.

The story of little Haloid holds the real answer. Wilson saw that demonstration in 1945. The Xerox bonanza wasn't born until fifteen years later, when the 914 copier hit the market, and knocked it sideways. McColough's doubts were thus amply justified. How many established managements would have made so instant a commitment to so long, arduous, and immensely difficult a development period, with an uncertain payoff—even if resources were abundant?

In Haloid's case, the 914 cost more to develop than all the profits earned by the company in the 1950s. One school of thought would declare this to be right and proper. It maintains that Haloid-style companies are the only places where Xerox-like breakthroughs can be expected. If that were so, it would be a tremendous indictment of the large corporation. But it isn't true. The creativity of the bigger businesses where most managers work is constrained by people who have the freedom to unleash it—and freedom under discipline is the key that can unlock the latent powers of American and other Western businesses. McColough knew this totally—yet his own corporation proved how well founded were his fears of the opposite.

It was McColough's inspiration to set up the Palo Alto Research Center to take the next stride forward in what then wasn't even called "information technology." The team brought together at PARC, by serendipity and brilliant personnel selection in equal proportions, identified and solved all the technological and conceptual problems that inhibited the production of the personal computer—as yet an unnamed dream. The PARC team went far beyond the Wang word processor, whose smash-hit debut in 1976 made it perfectly clear that office machinery, like accounting and scientific equipment before it, was certain to acquire electronic brainpower.

But the PARC scientists didn't know how to cope with the inertia and obstructionism McColough had feared. In a brilliant study, *Fumbling the Future*, Douglas K. Smith and Robert C. Alexander delineate the awful process which justified their subtitle: "How Xerox Invented, Then Ignored, the First Personal Computer." Demonstrated successfully at a "Futures Day" at Boca Raton in 1977, that computer, the Alto, was never put on the market—not by Xerox, that is.

In 1979, a very young millionaire named Steve Jobs, the creator of Apple Corp., visited Palo Alto and was deeply impressed. He is supposed to have asked, "Why isn't Xerox marketing this? You could blow everybody away." In 1983, first with the Lisa, and then with the Macintosh, Apple "replicated many features invented at Xerox." It was McColough's vision: he could have blown everybody away, but what was blown away was the chance to create a second business bigger even than Xerox's first breakthrough.

And Peter McColough was in charge the whole way through.

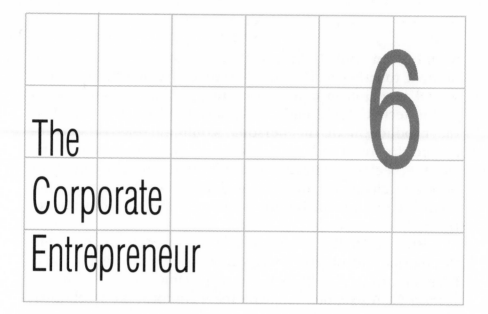

The Corporate Entrepreneur

6

An ancient Chinese curse, much quoted in editorials and other think-pieces, is "May you live in interesting times"— the point being that uninteresting times and countries (as Switzerland, for example, is alleged to be) offer better chances of living to a ripe and peaceful old age. In management terms, the curse should be rewritten: "May you live in turbulent times," which means that every management working today is cursed, for the times are surely the most turbulent business has ever known.

Turbulence is not an unmixed curse. It throws up many more opportunities than the steady state. One of the main reasons for the success of the opportunistic Japanese is that established Western rivals were undermined by turbulence that disturbed the foundations of their monopolies and quasi-monopolies. So far, the Japanese have known better how to exploit such turbulent developments as the eclipse of mechanical and electromechanical products by electronics, or the lowering of export cost barriers by the containerized transport revolution.

The opportunism they have deployed so successfully is another word for entrepreneurship: the great entrepreneur is someone who sees and seizes a great opportunity. So could the emphasis in management be shifting—in reality, not just lip service—toward that elusive animal, the corporate entrepreneur? Is the manager of the future the person who has most of the following qualities—isolated in a *Harvard Business Review* study by Geoffrey A. Timmons as the essential attributes of the entrepreneur?

1. A high level of drive and energy
2. Enough self-confidence to take carefully calculated, moderate risks
3. A clear idea of money as a way of keeping score and as a means of generating more money
4. The ability to get other people to work productively with you and for you
5. High but realistic and achievable goals
6. Belief that you can control your own destiny
7. Readiness to learn from your own mistakes and failures
8. A long-term vision of the future of your business
9. Intense competitive urge, with self-imposed standards

If that is the formula for the future manager, that's bad news for most present ones—for it's rare to find anybody in a seminar audience who owns to even six of the nine attributes (so convincing a list that I used them as the foundation for my book *The Supermanagers*).

But does increased turbulence really enlarge the need for entrepreneurial qualities? The important work done by Igor Ansoff on correlating corporate strategy with the degree of turbulence encountered by the firm turns out to have a great bearing on the answer to that question. The closer the fit, Ansoff says, the greater the success. Like the engineer he is, Ansoff has reduced the strategic success formula to sets of clear propositions, starting with the acute observation that return on investment (ROI) is no longer just the product

He is not, be it said, very impressed with the general results. In 1985, Deming observed that he saw "great advancement in spots." For every advancing American business, though, "others remain in the dark ages." To the extent that competitors ignore them, applying Deming's lessons is a powerful source of competitive advantage. To that same extent, it is a powerful source of national economic weakness. That much is obvious—but so is the muscularity and rightness of Deming's forty-year-old lessons.

Why were they ignored so long? The mystery doesn't only apply to quality control. Even when told how to improve operations, not marginally, but by great leaps forward, many managers don't; and even if advised of the virtues of forming a strategy, they don't; and even if they do, they don't take the necessary action to match the company's operations to its strategy.

In all this, Western sinners contrast shamingly with the Japanese, as the swift reaction to Deming's speech showed long ago, and as the Kepner-Tregoe consultancy has found to this day: its largest office outside the United States is in Japan, reflecting what Ben Tregoe describes as the "Japanese willingness to take whatever they can get hold of and improve it to obtain increased effectiveness." The mystery of why this willingness should be an Eastern specialty rears its head every time a management expert speaks or writes in the West.

The problem is that to accept radical change itself demands radical change—for starters. CEOs may know in their minds and hearts that they can no longer live in the past or manage in the present. They have to manage the future, now. Psychologically, however, they find it more comfortable to persist in believing that yesterday's solutions will solve today's problems. The obstinacy applies, most strongly of all, perhaps, to making that start, to changing the mind-set and the management style with all the sinewy rigor of Deming's philosophy.

The greater degree of discomfort lies not in change, but in resistance to change. That overwhelming truth can be seen more clearly in technology than in management, though its consequences are devastating in both. The annals are full of companies that (like RCA when the transistor replaced the thermionic valve) once led their markets, yet lagged in the next evolution of the technology. That compounds two errors: technical blindness and marketing inertia. What couldn't be afforded at a time when technology was moving relatively slowly must be ruinous in an age of accelerating, compressed change.

As the great innovator Konosuke Matsushita once sadly observed, "Today the same day you put a new product on the market it's out-of-date." That's what managing the future means in the simplest terms: having the next product ready when the new wonder is only being launched. More, it means drastically shortening time lags, so that if tomorrow should be needed today, the company can not only cope but conquer. Both reducing process time and accelerating product programs demand radically changed attitudes and actions in general management.

You can't manage the future in so positive a way simply by extrapolating the past and the present. Those who try to manage the future that way must miss the benefits of change—for change is not threat, but opportunity. It must be true that in a market where tastes, buying power, technology, and sources of supply are unchanging, opportunities will be hard to come by and still harder to exploit. By the same token, in markets that are changing, or can be made to change, opportunities are inexhaustible.

Nobody can escape the tension inside a business between those who deny reality and those who accept it. The good manager is at odds with the good leader, even inside the same man: the first manages what has always had to be done, while the second tries the new, where the chances of error are greater—and more frightening. Like individuals, organizations easily become victims of habit and inertia. Both vices are readily swept aside by the kind of crisis that has precipitated massive turnaround operations in large companies in every country of the West. But who wants a crisis?

In less threatening circumstances, fear of the unknown and distrust of the unpredictable inhibit acceptance. Sunk cost (the emotional and/or financial investment in the past) is an understandable barrier to adoption of the new. If the sunk cost isn't forgotten, the whole company may sink. It doesn't matter that accepting change implies error. So what if action taken in the immediate past was wrong? So what if the leader shared in, or maybe was wholly responsible for, the obsolete mistakes? In a fast-fluctuating world, once-correct decisions will be rapidly falsified—and there's no managerial sin in that.

Reluctance to admit to error is a close neighbor to the entrenched self-righteousness that is intensified by increasing age, experience, and success. The more you persist in error, though, the worse the position must become. The Watergate style of Management by Cover-up will only work for a while. Its timespan has notably diminished at the same time as the long-term damage from covered-up management has dangerously increased.

Even when change has been successfully completed, its problems can intensify: companies easily backslide into the same complacency and error as before. But if the climate for continual change doesn't exist, the organization can't manage the future. IBM wanted to call its change program "coping with change"—but the very title, suggesting that change could harm its people, rings false. By coincidence or not, IBM has been hard pressed to achieve the change to which its top management pays ardent service, or lip service.

"Coping" is fine for the evolutionary, incremental change that will be adapted to and absorbed within the bureaucratic whale, but only revolution—sudden, stark, and strongly symbolized change—will defeat the bureaucracy. The latter is bolstered by fear of mistakes, more of which are probable in a situation of flux. That raises a dual problem for management—how to tolerate error without fatally weakening performance, and how to survive, and succeed, in spite of the errors being made. It isn't a question of damage limitation or averting failure, but of creating success—of succeeding, in part, *because* of errors: mistakes made in the cause of progress.

Systemic error, of course, has no payoffs. The inbuilt tendency (it seems to have happened at IBM) is for market-led businesses to degenerate into product-led ones—and, worse still, for out-of-date methods of producing and managing to be neither challenged nor replaced. Instead of keeping themselves up-to-date, senior managers regress to the roles they knew and loved. These tendencies can be enhanced by job-hopping. Like bees passing from flower to flower, the job-hoppers carry the same ideas, the same attitudes, the same received views from company to company, until the whole industry behaves in the same claustrophobic, shortsighted way.

The pressure to achieve short-term financial results has become a notorious source of shortsighted management: CEOs have intensified that pressure, even though strategic goals and strategic contributions, which may not show up in the short-term numbers at all, are plainly more valuable. But managers lower down can't make a strategic contribution if all strategy is reserved for the corporate summit—which isn't the way they order things in Japan. The essence of the Japanese model is admirably described in his book *Inside Japan*, by Peter Tasker, a Japanese-speaking financial executive:

> New strategies are usually developed by middle managers, adjusted in discussion with the people involved most closely, then taken to the top for approval and official adoption. Those who disagree or have been disadvantaged can expect compensation the next time round. It is an effective method of procedure, conducive to good morale.

To set that the other way around, failure to involve middle management is a highly effective way of creating poor morale. As Tasker notes, the Japanese have believed in consensus decision-making for a long time. In the seventh century, writing his famous constitution, Prince Shotuko advised: "In order to achieve harmony, individual judgments and actions should be forbidden, and discussion at all levels should be respected." The excellence of the principle is self-evident; putting it into practice requires the acceptance of what amounts to deeply radical change for the typical Western corporation.

Combined strategic operations are needed to cope with large and growing challenges. All managements, the Japanese no less than those in the West, are faced with saturation in established markets; they all must seek new avenues of future growth by searching for new and different kinds of business. Ben Tregoe says "that's a new thing" for the Japanese—but it doesn't exactly seem second nature in the West. Indeed, some Western Johnny-come-latelies are still pursuing the former, now obsolete Japanese strategy of only improving quality and reducing cost.

As Tregoe says, pursuing the wrong strategic vision efficiently is as bad as inefficiency—a condition that he and Charles Kepner started to analyze thirty-one years ago, with research into why some managers are more effective than others. Later research, published in 1980, sought to answer a deeper question still: how does top management go about strategic decisions? In many cases it doesn't. "Strategy is like sex," Tregoe has said. "When all is said and done, more is said than done." In addition to total abstinence, potentially dangerous confusions abound: thus, managers equate long-range planning with strategy—"a recipe for disaster," according to Tregoe, who states that LRP is how strategy is *executed*, not devised.

Nor will a "mission statement do it all." Like Deming, Tregoe is characteristically blunt; a "mission statement equals strategy no more than the man in the moon." He is equally scathing about off-campus strategy sessions: "They take the top group away for a weekend on a mountaintop—it never works." The accusing finger points at the upbringing of top managers. Having risen through operational roles, they lack experience in forming a strategy. Worse, they are hesitant to give up what's made them what they are today—

so they interfere in operations, while strategy is often mere reaction.

Learning how to create strategy, and implementing it with the full rigor of Deming's teaching, isn't easy. It's the potential toughness and pain which explain that otherwise inexplicable failure of managements to do what, in their hearts, they know to be right. But buying off pain in the present only accentuates it in the future—if there is a future. Those who truly make it at the top will do so by creating that future. They will find that the new management requires a different kind of toughness, intellectual strength coupled with human responsiveness, but generates far less pain in the process.

You can grasp the full and intimidating extent of the new demands on managers from an anecdote related by Aguayo. He tells of a group of American executives visiting Japanese plants that supply the auto industry. After being shown everything in the plants and having every question answered, one of the Americans was curious to know why the Japanese were so ready to reveal all their methods: "The Japanese executive replied, 'We know you won't adopt what you have seen here today, and even if you did, by the time you instituted everything, we will be ten years ahead of where we are now.' "

The American competitor who takes that statement as an unalterable fact is little better off than the noncompetitor who doesn't even try the new methods of the Deming Age. The American competitor who takes that statement as challenge and bugle call is in there with a chance—and will have behind him the powerful driving force of proving that Japanese wrong.

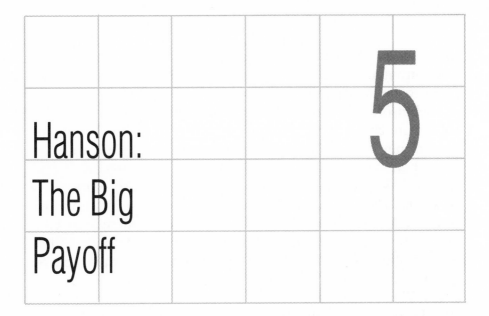

Hanson: The Big Payoff

If any successful group encapsulated the spirit of Ronald Reagan's era in America, and that of his admirer (and admired) Margaret Thatcher in Britain, it had to be Hanson Industries. Thatcher expressed her appreciation by ennobling both James Hanson, who masterminded the company from his English base, and Gordon White. The latter lord, starting with $3,000 of capital, built the North American interests to sales of $5.9 billion in 1989, with a return on stockholders' equity of 30.9 percent—topped by only thirty-nine of the Fortune 500 largest industrial companies.

Not to be outdone, the Hanson parent was the fourteenth most profitable of Britain's biggest 250 companies, according to *Management Today*, also with a 30.9 percent return on invested capital and (even more mouth-watering) a 1,608 percent rise in its share price over the previous decade. This amazing growth and profitability had been almost wholly acquisition-led: in the United States, starting with a $32 million fish processor called Seacoast, White cut his teeth

human beings." It "deals with the integration of people in a common venture" and is therefore "deeply embedded in culture." The enterprise requires "commitment to common goals and shared values." Every enterprise, too, "is a learning and teaching institution" that "must be built on communication and on individual responsibility." Then, neither "the quantity of output nor the 'bottom line' is by itself an adequate measure of the performance of management and enterprise. Market standing, innovation, productivity, development of people, quality, financial results—all are crucial to an organization's performance and to its survival."

Finally, "results exist only on the outside. The result of a business is a satisfied customer." As these quotes show, most other gurus are simply repeating the lessons of the old master (Drucker was born in 1909) in their own manner. But are management gurus condemned to be Cassandras—heard, but not heeded? Part of the trouble is that wisdom can become obsolete. Theodore Levitt became famous for his "marketing myopia" thesis, which warned against inadequate technological foresight and weak definitions of the business in which you're engaged. Myopia's moment passed, though Levitt has hit the headlines again by anticipating and elucidating the trend to global marketing.

Management by objectives, which sprang from a Drucker insight, had its moment of glory, and its time of decay, and so on. But teaching like Deming's and Drucker's doesn't truly date. Western managers who have become increasingly avid customers for the wisdom of the East (even seeking strategic lessons from an ancient guide to samurai swordsmanship) would do well to concentrate on the wisdom of the West, while bringing to bear one priceless Eastern power. That is the ability to listen, learn, adopt, adapt, and continually improve. They're the most important talents that anybody can teach, the easiest aptitudes for the willing to win—and the best tools with which to win.

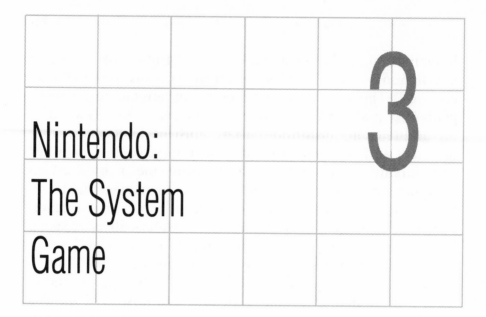

Nintendo: The System Game

3

The Age of Competition has seen some of the most startling marketing successes of all time, and none greater than those of Japanese companies whose reflexes are sharpened by incessant, furious competition at home. In that ferocious market, competing on price has always been discouraged. That has developed remarkable powers of competing along other dimensions of which Western rivals are only too well aware, and which they now have to master themselves.

As Professor Xavier Gilbert of IMD in Lausanne explains it, the first reaction to competition from the East was to raise quality. Once the quality edge gets blunted, though, firms turn to cutting costs, followed by prices, to keep down competition. As others take the same path, all contestants head into a commodity market, in which profit margins are enforced, not made. That's no fun for anybody. As a demonstration of how to gain and keep a competitive edge in the 1990s, Gilbert cites Nintendo, the computer games company, which competes not just with a product or products but with a whole business system.

Nintendo's company name means "leave it to heaven"; but little was left to chance during a growth phase that multiplied sales by ten times in ten years to $2.5 billion. Under its multibillionaire president, Hiroshi Yamauchi, the company had applied more and more sales appeal to its products and fastened a tighter and tighter grip on its market. The grip springs from total control over supply of hardware and software and distribution, covering a barely believable 80 percent of the world market in video games. That control, however, is achieved by systematic management at its most developed.

When it introduced its Famicon hardware, Nintendo selected a price point and quality standard and then created an entire network—design, production, software, retail, and after-sales services—so hugely comprehensive (the initial order for circuit boards was no less than 3 million) that competition was all but barred. The business system and thus the product were smash hits. Gilbert observes that "from the beginning, activities operated in network, not in sequence" as Nintendo selected its target, oriented its product, and rationalized the system.

Getting production, marketing, distribution, and the mass market aligned is what also saved the Swiss watch industry with the invention of Swatch. The first reaction to the Japanese blitzkrieg concentrated on cutting manufacturing costs, ignoring the realities of the business system. The factory accounted for only 22 percent of the cost to the customer. Given the extent of Japanese undercutting, bringing the cost of manufacture down to zero wouldn't have made enough difference, for 70 percent of the delivered cost occurred between the manufacturer and the point of sale.

When Swatch examined the system and shifted the point of attack (using a vastly improved and much more efficiently made product), it more than halved the cost of retail and wholesale distribution by moving to new channels—and brought the cost to the customer down by an eventual 55 percent. Nintendo's Yamauchi, who led the old family business from old-fashioned *hanafuda* playing cards into the new age, once told *Fortune*, "I don't really like video games," but he does like the Swatch game of combining low prices with high margins—and that tight control.

The magazine notes: "To earn a license, a software supplier must develop a game on spec, win Nintendo's approval, pay Nintendo to manufacture the cartridges, bear the cost of marketing—and agree not to supply the game for other makes of machine." What Yamauchi can't control, however, is the market reaction. The success of Swatch in the final analysis depended on the appeal of switching watches from timekeeping to fashion accessory. In an even more fashion-conscious industry, Nintendo is at unavoidable risk of going out of fashion.

The main visible dangers are that its hold might be rocked by rival products that suddenly steal the market's fancy—or the whole fashion might fold. But any rivals will still have to buck that system. Yamauchi had started extending into the adult market, into second-generation Super Famicon hardware, into information networks, into Europe, and possibly into education early in the 1990s. The true measure of the intensity of modern business pressures, though, isn't Nintendo's strength, nor those new opportunities just listed, but the way in which the weaknesses and threats, for all its systematic disciplines, have come to the fore.

The share price halved from the August 1990 peak, double the fall of the Tokyo index, not because of bad news, but because of fears of future ill tidings. Would Super Famicon pick up the torch from a faltering Famicon? Was Super Mario, Nintendo's video hero plumber, losing his mass-market appeal? In an earlier era, the questions would have ended right there. A company like Atari, zapped by the collapse of a previous video hit, had nothing on which to fall back. It was awfully managed; Nintendo is the opposite.

Its risk exposure, despite leaving nothing to chance, is the result of endemic change. Where previous winners, many of them still today's great brand names, could expect long and unbroken runs, latter-day champions climb mountains from which it is easy to fall. Another Japanese president,

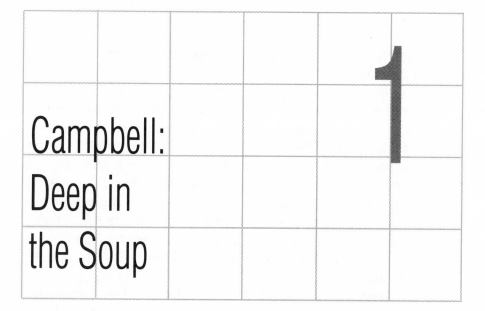

Campbell:
Deep in
the Soup

The best Japanese companies, no matter how great their success, have continued to seek enlightenment and improvement with indefatigable zeal. But Western management can be equally zealous for new lore. At Campbell Soup in Camden, New Jersey, for instance, the company took to heart W. Edwards Deming's powerful teaching on quality (Part II, Chapter 4). The company had soon sent 210 senior people to the Deming seminar (which lasts four days), dispatched 55 more people to university training in the necessary statistics, and given 2,000 hourly workers a four-hour quality introduction.

Author Mary Walton doesn't report what this four-year program did for Campbell's costs or quality—but it didn't save the company from deep trouble. In its 1989 financial year, profits were only $13.1 million on sales of $5.7 billion. Dissident members of the Dorrance family wanted to sell; and the last patriarch's successor was abruptly changed. The ousted CEO, R. Gordon McGovern, had brought avid enthusiasm for new management thinking to bear, but to no personal avail.

Not only did Campbell embrace the Deming method under his aegis; McGovern was also inspired by the "intrapreneur" creed, whose best-known advocate is author Gifford Pinchot III. Fifty general managers were told to run fifty business units independently and entrepreneurially in the spirit of yet another book—*In Search of Excellence*. That all sparked a new product splurge: 334 in five years. Yet in January 1990, *Business Week* reported that while the "mainstay condensed-soup line has been losing market share for years . . . new recipes haven't come along fast enough to keep earnings hot."

The best you can say for the results of all that management lore, then, is that without it Campbell might have been even deeper in the soup. That's a very downbeat conclusion for such an upbeat philosophy. What went wrong?

For the answer, turn to another guru, Igor Ansoff, the father of modern strategic planning. As reported in Part I, Chapter 6, research has left him convinced that the key to survival, success, and high profits, in any business, is the closeness of fit between that business and its environment. The degree of "turbulence" in the environment determines how rapidly and continuously the company has to adapt its strategies. Today, turbulence is very difficult to escape: get out of step with the environment and you suffer rapidly in consequence.

Campbell's new product program can't have been properly focused on the turbulent marketplace. Rather, such a plethora of new products must have created internal turbulence of a massive nature. And that sagging share in condensed soups quite plainly indicates strategic mismatch. Hearing the right message will merely palliate the damage if you're doing the wrong things in the right way: do the right things the right way, and the ideas of the gurus will return your investment a thousandfold.

The role of the CEO, though, isn't to act as conduit for the thinking of others: it's to be a thinker himself, and to stimulate thought throughout the company. The tragedy of Campbell's is that the business is fundamentally sound, both in its product line and in its tradition as a family firm. The dissension of the Dorrance clan and its alienation from the executive management robbed the company of that powerful motivation, carrying right through to multinational scale, which family ownership and personal identification can uniquely provide.

Families also have disadvantages. Campbell's seems to have fallen prey to some of the drawbacks, which notoriously include autocracy (and its aftermath), inbreeding, nepotism, difficulty in recruiting able outsiders, and (all too often) diminishing commercial drive over the years. According to a study by accountants Stoy Hayward and the London Business School, the nays have it: the average life of a family business is only twenty-four years, and only a fifth last beyond the second generation. Yet many of today's giants, with or without the founding family on the premises, haven't lost the founding drive.

In Campbell's own industry, close rival H. J. Heinz earned thirty-two times the former's 1989 net income on sales only slightly higher. Under Irish CEO Tony O'Reilly, a hard-driving exponent of incentive-led management, Heinz raised its earnings per share by 15 percent annually between 1979 and 1989; Campbell's earnings *fell* by an average of 21 percent. Even before the latter's calamitous 1989, Heinz was earning twice as much on shareholders' equity. The Heinzes showed more wisdom than the Dorrances in choosing the executives to whom they entrusted their wealth.

In 1989, O'Reilly was fourth on food's key statistical test, net sales margin. The three firms ahead of him have an interesting link with each other and with Heinz. They were led by McCormick's under CEO Charles P. McCormick, Jr. ("Spice scion is cooking up bigger market share, higher profits," according to *Business Week*); Wrigley, led by William Wrigley, Jr. ("Continues to chew up competition with inventive marketing, clever pricing and new products"); and Kellogg under a thirty-nine-year veteran, William Edward

LaMothe ("Nutritious recipe: High margins pay for spending on new products, efficient plants, snappy marketing").

All four are family foundations, two led that year by family members, two not. The entrepreneur's great task, after maintaining the enterprising breakthrough, is to establish an organization that will not only serve all immediate purposes, but outlive the entrepreneur, and grow and develop as it does so. In that last sentence, substitute CEO for entrepreneur, and you have the essence of the chief executive's true role for the 1990s and beyond.

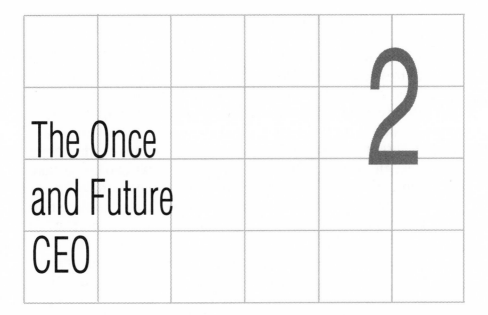

The Once and Future CEO

I s there any point in writing about the chairman as distinct from the chief executive, or asking whether they should be one and the same? In the interests of pure research, I was once going to tabulate how many of America's top chief executive officers, as listed in the *Business Week* executive compensation scoreboard, were also chairman. Statistical effort proved unnecessary. Page after page was filled not only by the legend "chmn & CE" but in many cases (just to rub it in) by "chmn., pres. & CEO." It might be better to plump for the title "supreme commander" and have done with it.

The title "chief executive" has gathered currency remarkably thick and fast: in the United States, not that long ago, the shots were mostly called by the company's "pres." or "president." Then, presumably through the endeavors of the management consultants from whom most newspeak flows, "chief executive officer" or CEO began its surge. The process worked in parallel with the growing conviction that the supreme executive role is primarily strategic. Tactics, or

in general and the nonexecutives in particular are supposed to have the final word. It's usually a word of assent, no matter how outrageous the amounts involved—like the $7.2 million the boss of Ford earned one fine year, inspiring a critic to say, "You reach a point of asking 'How high is up? How high is tolerable for a public corporation?' "

Much higher, evidently. The critic was Iacocca. A year later he pocketed $11.4 million, and the next year, not to be outdone by himself, made it $20.5 million. In 1990, for the third year running, Iacocca headed *Business Week*'s list of executives who gave shareholders the least for their pay: in 1986–88 he collected $41.9 million during three years when shareholders received only a 38 percent return: in 1987–89, the score was $25.2 million for a minus return to investors of 10 percent.

No doubt, Iacocca collected his reward without a murmur of boardroom dissent. The suspicion must be that companies would be better run if more dissent were possible—if the board ran the boss somewhat more, and, most important of all, if the boss ran the board a great deal less.

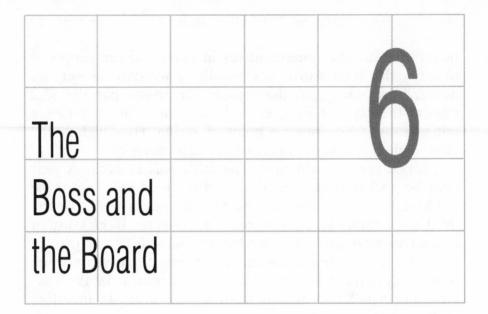

The Boss and the Board

6

The dominant boss's final opportunity to dominate his board is terminal: when a successor must be appointed. Henry Ford II spent much time and thought on the succession; after ousting Lee Iacocca, the eventual decision to step down in favor of Philip Caldwell was one of Ford's best. The family's stake is only a shadow of Henry I's total ownership; although the aura and the memory linger on (as does the presence, in the shape of younger and by no means quiescent Fords), that succession was possibly the last assertion of the dynastic rights of the Fords.

After all, Henry II's name, as he liked to point out, was over the door—for in the beginning was the Founder. Most of the world's great businesses (and, for that matter, most of the small and middling) trace back to a dominant figure or double-act, and much of the power and deference accorded to the boardroom boss has flowed down the generations from those creators of commercial genius. Often, they towered above contemporaries at a height barely imaginable today. Late-twentieth-century commerce abounds with monumental egos; yet, compared to J. P. Morgan, John D. Rockefeller, and Ford, today's giants, if not pygmies, are decidedly undersized.

The modern CEO doesn't need to fit that oversized mold. Great companies have great founders because it takes a driving genius, a prime mover, to animate an organization and move it bodily forward, to set the style and generate the ethos. The self-made entrepreneur in that classic style, a demon for work, highly paternal, immensely innovative, and deeply thrifty, can still create economic miracles: Japan has thrown up many such models. With luck and judgment, the prime mover finds a professional successor to move the business mightily on—like Ryuzaburo Kaku, who took Canon, the entrepreneurial creation of a medical man, from modest status to sales of $10 billion.

The Canon founder continued to preside as chairman of the board, just as Robert W. Galvin, a preternaturally successful heir at another $10 billion company, Motorola, wielded his very active influence as chairman of the executive committee, with a professional CEO (George Fisher) running the show. Those circumstances get nearest to the ideal relationship between boss and board. Cases like that of RJR Nabisco get farthest from it: when an exploitative top management includes the board among the exploited.

Exchanging ill-use for ideal isn't easy when the CEO, wrapped in the full panoply of an imitation founder, is chairman as well. Even then, if properly used, the board can be a powerful tool at the disposal of the chief executive for better purposes. Sir John Harvey-Jones, as part of his brilliant rejuvenation of the chemical giant ICI, slashed the board numbers and used the reduced team ably and deliberately. As he points out, though, only one person, the boss of bosses, "can develop the board as a collective organization, handle, select, and motivate its members, and manage its work."

That quotation from his book *Making It Happen* makes the real point: all is at the chief executive's option. If he so chooses, the board can become "purely ritual dancing," or at the other extreme, a place for "seemingly endless, fruitless debate." Plainly, any institution that is wholly at the mercy of one individual has no institutional power at all. Anyway, isn't the board supposed to monitor and to that extent control the actions of the chief executive? How can that be accomplished when in reality it's the chief executive who controls the board?

The views of powerful business leaders on the role of the board are as diametrically opposed as those last two questions imply. Take these two quotes: "I think the owners of the company should be represented by the directors. That has ceased to happen at a lot of companies where management dominates the board." So spoke Benjamin Rosen, the prolific venture capitalist whose five boards include that of growth star Compaq Computer (which, under nonexecutive chairman Rosen, showed its muscle by ousting the founding CEO, Rod Carion.)

Another *Fortune* interviewee thought quite otherwise: "The role of the board is not to be a contender against management. The role is to help management." The speaker here was Harold S. Geneen, who came to great fame as CEO of ITT, where nobody on the board, you may safely bet, said boo to the boss. On the other hand, the retired, nonexecutive Geneen was instrumental in booting out his own chosen heir, which the latter may not have construed as help.

Oustings are relatively uncommon; at major U.S. corporations, the topmost executive ranks have remained largely intact throughout the eras of scandal, predatory prowling, and absolute or relative failure. The main exceptions are the several CEOs (like those of RJR Nabisco and Revlon) whose golden parachutes opened so lucratively on takeover. One American academic regards the latter phenomenon as a gain for stockholders rather than the boss, because they positively encourage the management to drive the company into the arms of a purchaser, for a price that always exceeds the current stock market value.

This theory has somewhat strange connotations. Could

room, the structure and culture of senior management can be harmfully decisive. If Guinness and Distillers were isolated examples, that accusation couldn't be laid. But every bank failure in the United States produces another crop of nonexecutive directors who were apparently fiddling while their financial Romes burned.

The recurrent suggestion, in face of boardroom feebleness, is to strengthen the top through devices like greater investor intervention, or more and more powerful nonexecutives. That would only reinforce the top-heaviness that created the problem in the first place. The true renaissance of the publicly owned company will have to start much lower down, by liberating the energies of management below the top—the people running the part-businesses that are the whole business. That must include vital cores like, in these two cases, Scotch and stout. The Catch-22 is that nonexecutives, whose duty can best be fulfilled by that liberation, lack the power to bring it about.

The Nonexecutive Nonentities

4

When corporate raider Carl Icahn was trying and failing to bend Texaco to his will, he put forward some nominees for the board. One of them admitted, in the true spirit of the boardrooms that are supposed to be bygone, "I know very little about Texaco, but I don't think an outside director has to know the business." He didn't get elected. Did that matter, for good or ill?

Nonexecutives are only as effective as the information they get. If that comes from the executives (and what other source is there?), they can make it very hard to second-guess their decisions or criticize their actions. True, ignorance is no excuse: in 1985 all ten directors of one company were found personally liable for damages for an ill-spent two hours—that being the total time taken for the board to sell a railcar-leasing business in a hasty meeting (note) "dominated by the CEO."

The ten settled for $23 million, of which the purchasers paid $13 million and an insurance company coughed up the rest. At one point, not surprisingly, American insurers were running so scared of such suits that some premiums leapt by 9,000 percent in a year. Corporate chieftains fretted not only about the costs, but about finding anybody willing to serve. They needn't have worried. Awards of damages against directors are very rare, and the chieftains have found no difficulty in attracting outsiders (often their equivalents in other major corporations) to drink from the unpoisoned chalice.

The insurance premiums have settled down—but the issue hasn't. If you think the nonexecutive should provide better control over the executive and better results for the shareholders, how? The law is no answer. That $23 million settlement, for example, flowed partly from the fact that the directors hadn't read the sale contract before approving it. But if you're not a lawyer or an accountant, you will only spot truly gross sins in a legal document—even if you can understand it.

Every day directors put their names to long and tortuous verbiage in the hope that the professional advisers know what they're doing. That advice is the shareholders' true protection, on which, as the spate of suits against auditors shows, they notoriously cannot always rely. In most cases, the work of outside professionals is far more important than the contribution, or noncontribution, that outside directors make to the company's business.

No matter what their personal distinction, the role of the nonexecutive directors is likely to remain the same: low on power, and high on responsibility that can't easily be met. Given this fact, the critics are baying for the moon, if they want boards to become positive forces for better performance, urging companies on to prodigies of growth, efficiency, global enterprise, and innovation. You only have to think for a moment, or sit on a board for a minute, to know that the idea is nonsensical.

A recent recruit to the nonexecutive ranks, Robert Waterman, coauthor of *In Search of Excellence*, told me, when I interviewed him for *Management Today*, that he didn't think "we [at McKinsey] really knew" what goes on in the boardroom: how "groupthink" takes over as the great minds think (often wrongly) alike; how people "picked by the CEO and usually vetted by the succession" aren't likely to kick over many traces; how the clublike atmosphere militates against abrasive behavior, even if abrasion is needed.

The background of nonexecutives has a profound influence on their ability to be useful. Senior citizens associated with the company's past history, men who themselves run large groups, and representatives of minorities or the community are all hamstrung to various degrees: by their intimate past relationship with the present management, whose culture they share; by the wish not to rock somebody else's corporate boat lest others rock theirs; by simple lack of business experience; by absence of management muscle. The lone woman on the RJR Nabisco board was former Secretary of Commerce Juanita Kreps. *Barbarians at the Gate* records her brief attempt to bring sense to the issue of F. Ross Johnson's buyout plan:

"After a few moments, Juanita Kreps spoke: 'You know it seems a shame [that] we're forced to take steps like these, breaking up companies like this,' she said. 'On other boards I've been on there have been the same complaints about the stock languishing. The scenario elsewhere has been different. Managements look more to the future and beyond the immediate discounting of the stock. Why is it different here? Is it an issue of tobacco, with the decline in sales and the problems with the industry?' "

The lady's somewhat bemused question received a crisp, irrelevant and dismissive reply: " 'Juanita, I hear a lot of CEOs complaining about their undervalued stock, but I don't see them doing anything about it,' Johnson said. 'This is something you *can* do about it. The other guys are afraid to do anything about it.' " And that, apparently, was the end of that.

In more normal circumstances, nonexecutives seem to have power through manning the most influential committees of the board: those that decide on grave financial matters, on major developments affecting the company's future, or on the pay of executives. Some measure of the ineffectiveness of these committees lies in the enormous rise in average CEO pay since 1960 (from eleven times a schoolteacher's salary, according to *Business Week*, to sixty-six times). That partly reflects the scandalous amounts obtained by executives at the top of the tree (headed in 1989 by Craig McCaw's $54 million at the *profitless* McCaw Cellular).

It doesn't include those who fall off the tree, floating down under the golden parachutes (none more golden than Johnson's $53 million) to which the outside directors have meekly assented. The American system has simply not evolved any countervailing power on the board to match the rise of professional executive management. But the age of the boardroom sinecure may be ending. The outside director-ship has become notably less cozy for boards that preside over deterioration.

Stockholder suits for dereliction of duty, as noted above, may not cause much financial damage so long as directors are covered by insurance and the company against calamities. At Guinness, Ernest Saunders was ruined financially only because the family deserted its savior in his hour of greatest need. The deserters suffered nothing worse than embar-rassment—the noble earl had a particularly torrid time in the witness box. Still, harassment and the threat of professional damage should be enough to spur much sharper attention to the duties of the director.

An era of accelerating upheaval creates many more op-portunities for explosions that will suddenly load the nonex-ecutive directors with heavy fallout. Grumble and temporize as they may, they can't unload that weight. In the last resort, only the nonexecutive can act as bulwark of the nonexecutive interests involved in the corporation—including all those now named in the jargon as stakeholders: the public authorities, the community, the investors, the employees. The trouble is that last resorts come last. The existing mechanisms don't do enough to ensure that the nonexecutive applies a stitch in time.

Nonexecutive directors are ultimately there to ensure

that the chief executive fulfills what a Japanese counterpart would consider his prime responsibility: assuring the successful long-term continuity of the corporation. In the Western context, that makes it important that outside directors should be true professionals—not in some other role, but as nonexecutives. The development of the modern corporation has unfortunately given the occasional director increasing trouble in this respect. He can't keep up with the pace of corporate developments and information. He can't fairly be expected to play any constructive part in the boardroom as the load both of responsibility and of information increases.

In part this isn't entirely the amateur's fault. Existing methods of reporting and conveying information to the board are seldom suitable for sharp decision-making, or sharp awareness of what's actually happening inside the whale. But that sharpness is surely what the stakeholders (if they had both minds on the matter and voices) would demand from nonexecutive directors. The latter often don't even possess enough information to act on the data received. More often than not, they are compelled to be rubber stamps to the executives who supply the information and also determine how that information is delivered.

That can change radically with the electronic revolution. One day, quite soon, every corporation will have an executive information system (EIS) that will provide full corporate information, and the ability to dig down beneath it. The EIS sits on a desktop and responds to the touch of a few buttons. Some executives may well try to stop nonexecutives from turning these master keys to the corporate business. But that will pose in concrete terms, and in a challenge which can hardly be dodged, the issue of whether the nonexecutive element, and the board as an independent force, can really do its supposed job.

The whole company must be strengthened by moves to improve greatly the quality and quantity of the knowledge nonexecutives acquire about its affairs. Professionals with professional backup can be as helpful to the executive work of the company as the executives themselves, especially if their relationship *isn't* arm's-length. David Norburn, the director of the Imperial College Management School, reports that where nonexecutives represented the interests (and thus self-interests) of suppliers, outside investors, customers, or financiers, the corporate results were far better than at companies with boards composed of the disinterested great and good.

The professional nonexecutive director is already an established life form; it differs from the historical nonexecutive. In the first place, there's a clear limit to the outside responsibilities that the real pro can handle. Seven to eight boards is the practical extent of his useful workload—and that's pushing it. In the second place, to be any use, the pros must come expensive: the caliber of a person taken on in this function can't be any less than that of the people they are aiding and invigilating.

The fees offered to outside directors today are generally too low to attract the best talent. Not only are the fees too small, the opportunities are too casual. You know a man who knows a man (very rarely will it be more than a token woman). One study showed that 70 percent of such appointments were personal contacts—which simply means the bad old habit of filling the board with good ol' boys and gals.

The *de facto* situation may be moving closer to what the backers of new *de jure* solutions want to see. Nominating outsiders to represent specific outside interest groups—including women and minorities—presupposes a selection, probably not very large, of people who are qualified to serve. The executive directors, however, have the ultimate say. If they have any sense, they will turn more and more to outsiders who have a special interest or can offer specialist knowledge.

In the professional role, the nonexecutive director acts as a permanent consultant. Interestingly, the ex-McKinsey man, Robert Waterman, felt that his best contribution, and greatest insight into the corporate affairs, came from a couple of days' consultancy in addition to his nonexecutive duties. The CEO concerned was keen to perpetuate the arrange-

ple will react more strongly to action than words: they feel the hot breath of the short-term figures down their necks, and they know why their colleagues get fired—for not "making their numbers." Psychology operates in the same direction: just as managers told to report what they are doing to improve the business won't want the embarrassment (let alone the pain) of saying and doing nothing, so those in tough financial regimes don't fancy putting forward plans that will be savaged by the accountants and their superiors.

In the latter regimes, people aim only for targets they can hit—which may be a far smaller ambition than the company actually needs to achieve. In other words, reward systems must match the management needs of the company, not just its reporting and control requirements; and so, emphatically, must the information systems. In many companies, maybe most, historic accounts represent almost all the regularly available information. It's a palpable and potentially lethal inadequacy.

Managements that haven't taken radical approaches to escaping the chains of historic reporting may know well that the future, not the past, is where the destiny of the company lies. They may also know that the path to that destiny is paved with the intelligent use of the right, the real, and the rewarding information—including, but only among much else, the right figures. There's a danger, however: managers being bombarded with messages about the importance of information may forget the purpose of that vital commodity.

The aim of the electronic revolution is to replace that risk with the opportunity of turning unprecedented quantity and quality of data into a strategic armory. The new software makes full use of the new and increasingly powerful and convenient hardware to make management more effective. It can both improve internal operations and greatly raise the degree of responsiveness to the outside world. That means, among other things, moving away from the concept of being "market-led" or "customer-led."

Those phrases have become clichés, in the way of all good management ideas; every other corporate mission statement probably includes some such words. It has long looked sane to change the emphasis in this direction: companies that had always given the customer what the factory wanted to make, rather than what the customer wanted to buy, truly had to change. The models to imitate became companies like IBM—although the would-be imitators forgot that a *sales*-led company may think itself *customer*-led when (like IBM) it is nothing of the sort.

The phraseology, and the orientation, encourage the passivity you get by concentration on monthly historic reporting. Instead of making things happen, adopting a *proactive* stance, the "market-led" company *reacts*. Companies, like those managers with the radically minded boss, need to be forced to look forward, to anticipate market trends. Anticipation and forward thrust enable them to lead the market, not the other way around. That is the traditional role of the great entrepreneur.

People were buying portable radios before Akio Morita and his cofounder, Masaru Ibuka, came across the transistor and bought Sony the rights from AT&T for a paltry down payment of $25,000. They saw that the market would make a great lurch upward if they led it by taking advantage of the new technology to miniaturize the set. In just the same way, Morita led not only the market but his own reluctant marketing men when he sensed that, given the chance to buy their own portable hi-fi, millions would don the new lightweight headphones that made the whole dream possible.

Entrepreneurs lead markets by instinct. Managers inside companies are unlikely to have the same qualities of intuitive creativity. What instinct cannot provide, information can stimulate and nourish. Leadership is far more than market share, for example: future share depends not on the present penetration but on factors like relative perceived quality and service, on value for money comparisons, on which competitor (in reality, not in the management's own eyes) leads in innovation and technical specification. Without full information on how they rate today, managers can't even guess intelligently at tomorrow.

They also need full understanding of the trends that will shape the environment and the reaction of the markets. In many nonconsumer markets (and in some consumer industries) the mistake has been to identify the market with the buyers who actually place the orders. That error led the British aircraft industry, locked in overmatched competition with Boeing, into the trap of satisfying its monopoly domestic customer. Too late, the planemakers turned to meeting the needs of the real purchasers of their products—not only other airlines with different route structures and requirements, but the ultimate customers, notably the transatlantic and transcontinental traveler.

Markets have moved on far and fast since those days. That only increases the premium and the reward for getting ahead of markets and staying in that true lead. The danger of looking at the wrong numbers, and missing the right ones, is that the cycle of success, stagnation, crisis, rebirth, success, stagnation, etc. will peak at lower and lower levels—as at Philips.

After announcing that a fifth of the employees would lose their jobs, the new president hastily installed in July 1990, Jan Timmer, gave the London *Financial Times* a deeply depressing interview. "He was not interested in questions such as what kind of company Philips should be in the 1990s. The task now was to produce profits by improving stock control and making employees more aware of the competitive marketplace." You couldn't ask for a clearer example of either the journalist or the interviewee grasping the wrong end of the stick.

How could the employees be unaware of competition in industries like lighting, home electronics, and semiconductors? In Philips, the systems and signals alike had failed. Point the information systems of the company, including its bean-counting, in the direction of vitality and real growth, and not only will the managers get the right signals from the company, so will all its markets.

Toshiba: The Hidden Agenda

3

Look down on a Tokyo park in the very early morning, and you may see it dotted by people mysteriously performing their exercises in perfect time: somewhere in the park a peerless leader is leading the drill, which is transferred by those who can see him to those who can't, and so on, until all the exercisers are in perfect unison. That epitomizes the Japanese management approach, which has achieved such startling leadership in industries where, originally, the Japanese were led—and by large margins.

In the electrical industry, for example, the United States achieved leadership at all the beginnings. The inventions of Thomas Alva Edison spawned the industry's development all around the world, just as in a later era the semiconductor pioneering of Bell Laboratories and Silicon Valley moved the entire global industry into the new era of solid-state electronics. Yet in the 1990s only one U.S. electrical company is in the world top ten by size—the biggest, General Electric. Four of the others are Japanese; their combined sales are three times GE's.

The largest, Hitachi, close enough to GE for the latter's advantage to be wiped out by some unfavorable movement in the dollar, endeared itself to me by an ad campaign headlined, "The 2,000 years of Hitachi." That long view is echoed by what happened fifty years in Matsushita Electric's brilliant history. The great Konosuke Matsushita called his team together to celebrate their success over the previous fifty years and to discuss their strategy for surpassing that achievement in the next fifty—a period that he was very certainly not going to see unfold. He died in 1990, probably in perfect confidence about his company's worldwide encore.

You can't separate Japanese corporate strategy from these long-sighted visions or from the culture that permeates them. In their study *Strategic Control: Milestones for Long-Term Performance*, Michael Goold and John J. Quinn took a look at Toshiba to compare its strategic planning with that of Western companies, including GE, and found, for a start, that while there is a formal planning system, it doesn't create strategy.

Instead, "decisions are reached through collaboration between levels and represent a consensus between them. Building the consensus involves frequent informal meetings, subtle hints, and thorough staff work." In other words, there's a hidden agenda: strategy is inseparable from the culture of a company that (so its philosophy declares) "contributes to a richer and healthier life and to the advancement of society through the creation of new values based on human respect."

That lofty declaration meant, among other things, providing "staff members with the opportunity to realize their full potential and cultivate their abilities." Fine words, indeed: but, as the British say, fine words butter no parsnips. The Toshiba experience in Britain, however, shows how effectively the fine words are backed by deeds. Taking over a money-eating factory previously owned in partnership, but still working through a British chief executive, the company utterly changed the culture.

Out went the hierarchical canteens as uni-status dining

and uni-status hours, holidays, and pensions took over. Individual offices vanished. Everybody donned the same blue Toshiba jacket. In went Japanese ideas on good housekeeping. The new owners took it for granted, in Plymouth as at home, that production equipment would be the best available, that inventory levels would be rigorously controlled, and that financial management would be as neat and exemplary as the premises—repainting the factory was one of Toshiba's first and most symbolic acts.

That, too, is standard national practice. At Fort Dunlop, once the citadel of outdated British management practice, the Sumitomo tire company promptly instituted the four S's: *seiri, seiton, seiso*, and *seiketso*, or sorting, orderliness, cleaning, and cleanliness. The chairman (a Briton, note) commented: "Our factories have been cleaned up, and are kept that way, not by a team of cleaners, but by the workers themselves. Their machines have been painted in bright colors; and every item is allocated to its appropriate place."

The good housekeeping is of a piece with applying the "simple and obvious" (to quote the same Brit) to every aspect of the company: the same principles run all the way from the man at the machine to the boardroom strategist, from the stores to the labs. All are tied together at Toshiba by what Goold and Quinn call "a long-term vision for the company that looks forward into the twenty-first century but is primarily concerned with the next decade." Future changes in society, the economy, and technology are covered in a statement that maps out the aimed-for structure and mix of all Toshiba's businesses.

Brilliant breakthroughs, like the laptops that took Toshiba from nowhere in the global computer market to leading position in its fastest-growing and most profitable sector, are generally the work of project teams; they are set up "to convert broad ideas . . . into more specific plans." Toshiba's vision was first drawn up in 1984, but is subject to revision and updating. As Goold and Quinn comment, "The most important elements of control stem from a corporate culture in which people work together in teams to achieve shared

2. The customer is the judge of our quality. His or her opinion on our products and services is decisive.

3. Our quality goal is always "zero defects" or "100 percent right."

4. Our customers assess not only the quality of our products, but also the quality of our services. Deliveries must be on time.

5. Inquiries, offers, samples, and complaints must all be dealt with promptly and thoroughly. It is imperative that agreed deadlines be met.

6. Each and every employee in the company contributes toward achieving our quality goals.

7. All work must be without defects from the very beginning.

8. Not only defects themselves must be eliminated, but also their causes.

9. Demand the highest quality from our suppliers, and support them in adhering to our mutual quality goals.

10. We have introduced numerous and proven methods to identify defects at an early stage. These methods must be rigorously and consistently applied.

11. Ensuring that our quality goals are achieved is an important management duty.

12. Our quality directives are compulsory.

That last word means what it says. Bosch believes that its middle and top management have been converted to the total quality cause, but that the remaining problem is with the motivation of the worker on the shop floor. As American companies have found, that demands a change of culture. That's where Manger feels his Japanese competitors have the advantage: "When I visit a Japanese shop floor I feel the workers are more motivated than in some of our own plants." No doubt that's partly the result of those eleven languages—but there's more to the problem than that.

If the deficiencies are felt deeply in a company like Bosch, where "total quality has been part of our philosophy" from the beginning, and which believes its founder created TQM ("although at the time it was not known as this"), the problems, and the necessity, must be enormous in the more typical firm. Bosch wants to go from "an acceptable failure rate of half a percent or so to zero defects": many companies still have 20 percent of rejects and rework: for them zero defects is as far away as the moon, if not Mars.

But the journey must be started. Outside Japan, "there are still people who believe that zero defects is impossible, that it costs too much even to attempt, and that it is much more economical to allow a certain failure rate and just replace the failed parts to your customers." Actually, zero defects isn't realistic, but that makes no difference to Manger's argument: "Let's come close, twenty defect parts per million, ten defect parts per million, without the target of zero defects we will never get there." And there is where the Western company, like it or not, has to get—and can.

Quality's Total Impact

Two elements are immediately prominent in Robert Bosch's quality manifesto. First, improved value for the customer is both objective and foundation of Total Quality Management. Second, this is a "hard" discipline, not a "soft" statement of aspirations. That truth hasn't been seized by skeptics who wonder whether TQM isn't just another passing fashion, like Management by Objectives, say, or long-range planning, that will have its day and then make way for the next fad.

The Japanese have been practicing their versions of TQM for forty years now. Not only is that far too long for mere fashion, but the results obtained by the Japanese are far too good for anybody to ignore. Indeed, that's what has inspired the upsurge of interest in total quality on both sides of the Atlantic. In the case of Hewlett-Packard, it was especially hard not to heed the message: in 1982 its Yokohama offshoot was the winning division competing for the Japanese Deming Prize, the world's premier quality award.

The prize was based, as always, on hard and hard-totrusted marketing objectives are valuable—especially, as noted, the last. But Sir Colin Marshall, the chief executive of British Airways, pointed out in a letter to the *Harvard Business Review* that understanding complaints isn't anything like enough. Far better to stop them arising in the first place—because (see above) you always lose a percentage of complaining customers, and "it is a well-known business maxim that it is far, far harder—and more costly—to win back a dissatisfied customer than it is to win a new customer."

That only enhances the argument for emphasizing service. The magazine *Car & Truck Dealer* found that 68 percent of car buyers switching makes (oddly enough, the same percentage as that of dissatisfied and departing Canadian customers quoted above) do so because they are disappointed in service and treatment. That compares with a mere 14 percent who switch because of the product—thus seemingly implying that products don't count. But the statistics conceal a terrible trap: you can't cover up product deficiencies by wonderful service, and that 14 percent means far more customers than you can afford to lose.

Merely reflect on that disappointing launch of the new Ford Escort in Europe. While pouring effort into quality of product, quality of working life, and quality of dealerships, Ford lost European product leadership to General Motors. Ford has paid the price of a fall in UK market share from the 30 percent of the early 1980s to 24 percent, plus a severe drop in vital European profits. It's the same point as that highlighted by the pre–Gulf War travails of the Scandinavian airline SAS under CEO Jan Carlzon. He won worldwide fame for his enunciation and execution of quality-of-service principles—but no one dimension of the business holds the key to eternal marketing success.

Everything must be continually got right—unless nobody else is in the game. Carlzon unblushingly told his employees that "we make a profit where we face no competition and we make losses where we face competition." Only brilliant ideas brilliantly sustained are likely to produce the first state in these tough and toughening times; but the second state is simply unacceptable, and there's a simple way to avoid it.

Never rest on your laurels in any aspect of the market—if you want to keep any laurels. Apply that philosophy to every aspect of the brand, and you are likely to make good and growing profits even where you face tough competition. Which is what, today and tomorrow, you are more than liable to get.

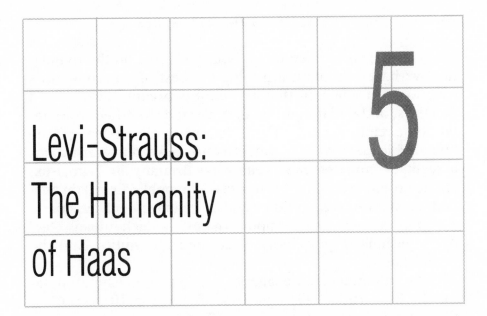

Levi-Strauss: The Humanity of Haas

5

The blue jeans of Levi Strauss have circled the world, or at least its *derrières*. The company could yet become as famous for its management as its denims. After a relatively unhappy episode as a public company, Levi Strauss thankfully took itself private in 1985. Since then profits have risen fivefold to $272 million on $3.6 billion of sales. That's enough to satisfy most managers' aspirations—but that word has a special meaning at Levi's.

It boasts an "Aspirations Statement" that is quite a read, beginning: "We all want a company that our people are proud of and committed to, where all employees have an opportunity to contribute, learn, grow, and advance based on merit, not politics or background." The words continue in the same humane vein: "We want our people to feel respected, treated fairly, listened to, and involved. Above all, we want satisfaction from accomplishments and friendships, balanced personal and professional lives, and to have fun in our endeavors."

The statement then talks about "building on the foundation we have inherited: affirming the best of our company's traditions, closing gaps that may exist between principles and practices, and updating some of our values to reflect contemporary circumstances." There follows a discussion of the "type of leadership . . . necessary to make our Aspirations a reality," covering new behaviors, diversity in "age, sex, ethnic group, etc." (not businesses—the public Levi's diversified dismally), recognition, ethical management practices, communications, and "empowerment"—which means "actively pushing responsibility, trust, and recognition into the organization."

As an empowered example, the sewing machine operators at Blue Ridge, Georgia (one of the top 10 percent of the company's plants) were set production goals, absenteeism rates, and safety standards and left to make their own economies or productivity improvements. Chairman Robert Haas reported in an interview with the *Harvard Business Review*, "They're taking initiatives and making things work better because it's in their interest and they don't have to be told." The "interest" was a half share in any savings, with the result that Blue Ridge became "one of the top two plants—after only nine months in the new program."

Haas also cites the success of Dockers—"a brand-new segment in the casual pants market," which became a half-billion-dollar line without an initial business plan, thanks to managers "who saw an opportunity . . . and made commitments for production that were greater than the orders they had in hand." The boss's conclusion that Dockers wouldn't have "happened before this more collaborative, open style of management" can be neither proved nor disproved. Plenty of entrepreneurial successes have been rammed through unplanned by managers as collaborative as Joseph Stalin and in cultures as easygoing as ancient Sparta.

One driving tycoon even expressed his own equivalent of the Levi Strauss "Aspirations Statement" under the title "Ten Spartan Rules." They run as follows:

1. Create work for yourself; don't wait for it to be assigned to you.
2. Take the initiative in performing your job, instead of playing a passive part.
3. Grapple with big jobs—petty tasks debase you.
4. Choose difficult jobs. Progress lies in accomplishing difficult work.
5. Once you start a task, never give up—complete it, no matter what.
6. Lead those around you. Leading others instead of being led makes a big difference in the long run.
7. Have a plan. A long-term plan engenders perseverance, planning, and effort, and gives you hope for the future.
8. Have self-confidence. Otherwise your work will lack force, persistence, and even substance.
9. Use your brain to the fullest degree at all times. Keep an eye on all quarters and always be on the alert. This is the way we ensure satisfactory service.
10. Don't be afraid of friction. Friction is the mother of progress and the stimulus for aggressiveness. If you fear friction, you will become servile and timid.

What nation spawned this exhortation to self-motivation and abrasive effort? And what kind of business did its author command? Neither question is easy to answer: the business is advertising, which is more commonly associated with free-and-easy creativity than the lash of the hard taskmaster. As for the nation, it's Japan. The credo is that of Hideo Yoshida, who built the Dentsu agency into the largest in the world.

The Spartan rules are a useful antidote to the sentimental idea that Japan's corporate cultures achieve their result through humanely shared values: they are also cultures of hard work and harder words. Not for nothing did Kuniyasu Sakai, writing in the *Harvard Business Review* (November-December 1990), headline his article "The feudal world of Japanese manufacturing." For instance, when as a small supplier he visited the president of a big company, his sole client, "to profess my sincere desire to support his company's growth and to ask for more work," Sakai got this reply: "Your words are like an expression of affection from an ugly woman."

In the West, which is less able than Japan to swallow the bad and the ugly along with the good, dictatorial and harsh corporate cultures are notoriously short-lived. Western leaders like Haas are trying to create enduring and developing societies by moving well beyond the expression of humane corporate values into fitting deeds: matching empowering aspirations with empowering actions. At the end of one worldwide management meeting, Haas "held up the Aspirations Statement and ripped it to shreds." He told those present to "think about what you want for the company and what kind of person you want to be in the workplace and what kind of legacy you want to leave behind."

The boss told them that "if the result happens to be the Aspirations, that's fine." Otherwise, they were to feel free to form their own principles, and he would "go with whatever you come up with." That grand gesture was highly symbolic—I'd be astounded if Haas's offer had any result other than endorsement of the Aspirations, for they express most enduring forces. Its key words are "building on the foundations we have inherited" and "affirming the best of our company's traditions." For a member of the Haas family, which started the business in 1850, that's easy to say. But what about late starters?

The
Value
of Values

6

Every businessman—including Robert Haas of Levi Strauss—knows the sovereign importance of the bottom line. That's where the profit, if any, is kept or recorded. But where's the top line? In accounts, that dignity is accorded to turnover or its equivalent. But the true top line isn't measured or reported in monetary numbers, though its contribution in financial terms may be immense. That top line is "value."

The word is vague or "soft" enough to curl a hard-nosed manager's lip, and the actual words used in "value statements" would score no points either. Or would they? A study of twenty companies that, for at least a generation, have lived according to a value gospel (of which the Levi Stauss "Aspirations Statement" is a good example) found a twenty-three-fold growth in net income. That compares handsomely with the two-and-a-half-times rise in America's gross national product over the same period.

The *Harvard Business Review*, in an editorial, observed

dropping extraneous activities to concentrate on some chosen field.

The final stage was to build on these foundations by *development* of the business, investing in organic growth and/ or acquisitions. After which, the cynic would say, the sixth stage would be another menopausal attack, another slow-down, another crisis, and here we go again. But there's another valuable clue in the Kalchas research. Some of the thirty-two takeoffs were more successful than others: share prices of the A Group over five years increased by 21.2 percent annually against 16.2 percent for the B Group and 14.3 percent for the market. That added up to the As performing against the market over three times better than the Bs.

Nor was this just stock market froth. Earnings per share growth for the As outstripped the Bs by even more—30.2 percent per year against 16.5 percent. While the Bs doubled their EPS over the five years, the As came close to quadrupling. Obviously, if some secret ingredient X explains the difference, it must be mighty magic. Michael de Kare Silver of Kalchas points to one important part of the secret recipe: acquisition policy. Buying other companies is a favorite corporate pastime, but the how could be as important as the what. To be precise, many smaller acquisitions, good; bigger single acquisitions, not so good.

Remember, however, that the consultants were only looking at successful companies: making too many small buys has laid low many a less adept management. If you know what you're doing, though, the small strategic buy, designed to reinforce organic growth, appears to offer fewer hazards to fortune than the great leap forward—especially if the leaper buys a whole company. When *Business Week* looked at the ten best and worst deals of the 1980s in the United States, 90 percent of the duds were whole-company buys; the wows were either purchases of divisions from less competent hands or (which comes to the same thing) buys of whole groups, swiftly dismembered to leave only the object of strategic desire.

The four cases where the purchaser bought only part of

a much larger company were Grand Metropolitan's purchase of Heublein from RJR Nabisco, Rupert Murdoch's $2 billion acquisition of TV stations from Metromedia, UAL's snip buy of Pan Am's Pacific routes, and Wells Fargo's removal of the Crocker National monkey from the British Midland Bank's suffering back. The six other bests included Dow Chemical's selling off less promising medical products after it bought into drugs; General Electric's dropping huge chunks of RCA (for $2.5 billion); and Quaker Oats' getting swiftly up to $125 million of annual operating profits from Gatorade sporting drink, which cost a net $95 million after selling everything else in the deal.

The explanation for the success of these partial buys isn't magical. Buy a whole company, which in the dud cases was generally in a different business, and you may well be stuck with its culture, its top management, its shibboleths, and (more often than not) its plunge into awful results. The bigger the buy, moreover, the greater the financial damage done by disappointment. Those ten worst U.S. deals were on average 1.2 times the size of the acquirer; the best buyers acquired businesses averaging seven-tenths of their own size, before any of those instant disposals.

Where the good and great deals sought, got, and rapidly digested highly specific strategic gains, the bad deals ran the gamut. Rotten timing was the villain when Fluor bought a commodity business just before the 1982 prices slump. Its feat was emulated by Sohio when the oil company bought into copper. Strategic error led to Pan Am's buying National for its domestic routes and thus setting itself up for the loss of the valuable Pacific runs. And there was ludicrous overambition, as in Blue Arrow's purchase of Manpower Inc. The British buyers couldn't manage the twice-as-large American business, and they wouldn't leave it to those who could.

The good-buy guys only bought related companies, but absorbed them instantly into the culture and management of the new owners. They knew what needed to be done before the bid (because they had real strategic purpose), and they wasted no time over the next most important step—doing it.

Another way of describing the guiding light of these successes is focus. The single-product company has a rotten name, largely because of the risk of being zapped by competition and changes of fashion, with nowhere else to turn. But for single-product, read highly focused, and the story is very different.

A piece of research by Nat Sloane, also of Kalchas, shows that the larger the number of "primary business areas," the lower the stock market rating: from which it follows that the fewer businesses you are in, the more the market loves you. Since the market is by no means stupid (not all the time, anyway), there must be cause and effect, and there is. The more focused companies, with only one or two business areas, increased earnings per share over 1984–88 nearly twice as fast as the six-or-more-business diversifiers.

The damage done to the latter by themselves is measured precisely in the *Harvard Business Review* by two McKinsey consultants. They report what happened when an incoming chief executive reexamined acquisitions that had cost the company $700 million in purchase prices and $100 million in further net investment. "There was no doubt that the company had increased growth—but at considerable cost. In fact, the company's new business sectors had *reduced* shareholder value by more than $500 million. . . . shareholders would have been $500 million better off if the corporation had distributed cash to them."

The two authors, David L. Wenner and Richard W. Leber, are scornful of anything that doesn't add "economic value," which they define as "net present value of expected cash flow discounted at the cost of capital." Applying "shareholder value analysis" (SVA) answers "four fundamental questions":

1. *How well has the portfolio been doing?* (That's the question that threw up the $500 million *negative* value of the buys.)
2. *Does the company's planning make sense?* (In this case it didn't—because three businesses accounted for more than 90

percent of the company's total economic value, while the Dirty Dozen remaining contained 30 percent of the assets and devoured half the management's time.)

3. *How much better should the company be doing?* (If you look at ways to achieve the best economic value for each business, your attention is drawn automatically to ways of improving operations, cutting costs, lowering working capital, etc.)

4. *What should the priorities be?*

That last question can yield especially fascinating answers. The above company ran a series of alternative strategies through the computer, estimated and discounted the cash flows for each, and changed underlying assumptions one by one to see what were the "value drivers." The analysis showed that sales productivity was the most important driver: more, an aggressive growth policy was only the best choice if sales-force productivity really could be improved (as, in fact, it nearly always can).

Shareholder value analysis often only confirms what a half-blind management should have been able to see. To quote Grand Metropolitan, now the owner not only of Heublein but of many more of the world's best liquor brands, "We need market leadership and we can only get that in so many businesses." The point is so obvious that you wonder how any managements, no matter how menopausal, could possibly miss it—yet they do. Dunlop, while on its tragic way out of the tire business, had a fishhook firm; not to be outdone, Carrier Corp., lately clobbered by the Japanese in air conditioning, had the fish farm mentioned in Part VIII, Chapter 1. Perhaps they should have got together. Dunlop never did escape from its crisis, and fell to takeover, while Carrier collapsed into a profit slump.

An earnings collapse is one of the three main instigators of crisis, along with downturns of the entire market (which will also collapse profits) and hostile bids. The postcrisis stages of corporate takeoff are built into the corporate culture of the right company—starting with *review*. A couple of quotes gleaned by the researchers make the point: "We are reexamining our business strategy in some depth" and "we are looking again at everything we have taken for granted." These are highly beneficial activities even for a very healthy company, and they may well lead to the next phase identified by Kalchas: *restructuring*.

That has mostly meant closing down and laying off. Ensuring that the business structure fits the long-term strategy will always involve chopping and changing: they are always far better done in good times than in bad. But what truly matters comes next, after restructure: not rebuilding, but *building*. It's not enough to escape from menopausal drift by getting a proper focus—although that's vital: Guinness made no sense at all as an anything-goes conglomerate run by booze barons, but is logically secure as a booze empire managed by marketing supremos.

Many of Wall Street's disgraced favorites, the former entrepreneurial stars of yesteryear, made the same error. Like Field Marshal Montgomery, who went a bridge too far at Arnhem, the hotshots often made one acquisition (a big one, note) too many. Relatively early in their careers, they achieved an unnoticed midlife crisis: behind the acquisitive growth lay inadequate organic expansion. For the driving truth is that acquisitions and original businesses alike can succeed only if their underlying growth is good enough—and the fact that all organic supergrowth comes to an end is the fundamental cause of the profits plateau.

Buy a supergrower at the crest of its wave—like Xerox acquiring the now dead and gone SDS computer business for one-third of its own capitalization—and desperate efforts to justify the buy through extravagant expansion may well (as then) utterly destroy the purchase. If you can buy half a wonder product's world rights, outside America, for £300,000 (as Britain's Rank Organisation did with Xerox), the problem naturally doesn't arise. But most corporate purchases are fully valued, if not overvalued—and thus only new growth, achieved in the *development* phase, ultimately justifies the buy.

Even that's putting carts before horses. The midlife miracles mostly make buys to sustain the organic growth being achieved in their existing businesses. That selfsame Rank, after dropping more than one hundred now unwanted buys in three years, made several small purchases of less than £40 million apiece in pursuit of the policy of "strengthening core market positions via acquisition." Another midlifer put the issue another way when remarking that "we only need to make small acquisitions because our organic growth is so strong." Said another, "Our acquisitions were carefully planned and complementary to businesses we know about."

What businessmen say and what they do, of course, are not necessarily the same thing. One man's "complementary" activity may be another man's unrelated nonsense. The same subjective difficulty affects even "strong organic growth." How much depends on price rises, rather than adding value for the customer? What's happening to market share, accurately measured? What proportion of the rise merely or mainly reflects market conditions—like the monetary overexpansion and lax controls that, far more than their financial genius (if any), created Wall Street's recent (or late) heroes?

The right company's management never deceives itself with good figures, or glib phrases, or anything else. It is only interested in real growth for the corporation, with management's own pay packets and prestige as secondary considerations. When it goes shopping for growth it makes sure that it buys the right company, in the other meaning of "right." And having bought a business, it manages it in the only right manner—to achieve major organic growth. That's the way, whether or not the firm is post-proprietorial, like Time and Disney, to achieve the best of all solutions to the midlife crisis. Don't have one.

delegating more authority; open all jobs to all comers, right up to the highest parental level. That's good multinationalism and excellent management alike. The theory of delegation, nationally or multinationally, is to have each operation managed by the most able and suitable person. If that man or woman doesn't make the decisions, but the boss does, where's the delegation?

You only need to look over managers' shoulders and countermand them if they're no good. Doing that makes them worse; second-guessing leads to third-rate management. The fact that, thanks to the IT revolution, the higher ranks of management can now be far better informed puts more ammunition behind their right and duty to say (with due discretion) what they think. They also have the right and duty to remove and replace managers whose decisions and actions fail. That's power enough for any sensible purpose. The right to interfere with the exercise of delegated responsibility is a contradiction in terms: responsibility without authority is no responsibility at all.

Implementing this truth demands more tact and self-restraint than most multinational CEOs habitually show. Part of a multinational business can only galvanize or sustain the whole (as have the European operations of Compaq and Apple) if the branches have equality with the center. Greater transnational equality is the inevitable trend, the only one that makes sense. Both sides gain greatly, whatever their nationality, by becoming one side, peopled by borderless managers who match Kenichi Ohmae's "borderless world."

One giant group selects its candidates for this role by applying the acronym SMILE. The corporation seeks Skill, Management ability, Internal flexibility, Language facility, and Endeavor (described as vitality, perseverance in the face of difficulty). Significantly, SMILE comes not from a Western company but from Matsushita Electric. The Japanese have achieved the impossible in world markets by their philosophy as much as by their products. Given their inherent multinational advantages, Westerners can achieve even more.

The Washington Post: What Katy Did

3

Many managers, some with genuine modesty, others with false, have declared that their CEO predecessors have given them (to quote one example) "everything but an easy path to follow." Very few have said it of a woman, for very few have had that opportunity. That quote, however, was uttered by the heir apparent at the Washington Post, Inc., one of the world's most deserving media groups. The heir was speaking of his mother, Katherine Graham, which doesn't detract from the sincerity of the tribute or the value of her achievement, corporate and personal.

The personal distinction can be gauged from one truly hard fact. At the start of 1989 only three CEOs out of the 1,000 companies ranked by *Business Week* as America's biggest were female—and one of those (Liz Claiborne) had founded her own company. As for Graham, she inherited her job on the suicide of her husband, Philip, who in turn had taken the mantle from Katy Graham's father, Eugene Meyer. A year later only Mrs. Graham was numbered among the elite 1,000, Claiborne having made a graceful exit. Not a single professional female executive had made it into the male Valhalla as the century's last decade began.

Yet nobody could deny Graham's professionalism or her success. Where women have stepped into business, either as principals (like Claiborne or Helena Rubinstein) or as consorts or widows, they have often showed brilliant ability. In researching my book *The Age of the Common Millionaire*, I noted an extraordinary number, far higher than probability would suggest, of other media widows. These women, just like Graham, had taken hold of newspaper, broadcasting, and magazine empires after the deaths of their husbands and outperformed them.

Helen Copley, the queen of the nine-daily Copley Press, credited with injecting strong commercial management into papers like the *San Diego Union/Tribune*, was a staunch tidier-up of holdings and a conservative empire builder. Dorothy Stimson Bullitt was the first person to open a TV station in the Northwest and the prime force behind King Broadcasting; in an uncanny parallel with Katherine Graham, Mrs. Bullitt took over her father's bequest on her husband's death. Since that was in 1932, the King expansion has to be her doing.

That's also true of Oveta Culp Hobby's broadcasting interests, added to the *Houston Post* (later sold), which she inherited from her spouse, a former Texas governor. The billion or two value of these female-dominated family holdings is partly fortuitous: newspapers, magazines, and broadcasting have made easy money for many males of no conspicuous management ability—like Walter Annenberg, former ambassador to the Court of St. James's, who pocketed an out-of-this-world $3 billion from Rupert Murdoch for interests topped by *TV Guide*. That doesn't, however, invalidate the remarkable success of those four media queens.

But is their success really "remarkable"? That can only be true if you start from the absurd proposition that women are unlikely to excel in business. The media widows were the forerunners of what are now hundreds and will be thousands of successes, and not only in the media. From the moment that a large pool of ambitious, educated women, interested in the diverse activities known as management, came into being, their progress into executive power has been inevitable. Timing is the only issue left in doubt.

The media have provided the perfect opening for talents like Katherine Graham's because of the peculiar structure of enterprises like newspapers. They maintain a generally clear division between editorial and business (the latter being the side, as the columnist A. J. Liebling once tartly observed, where they keep the money). The high cash flow of papers, paid for by customers on the spot, has made the preservation of proprietorial rights much easier to finance. With no need for deep reserves of management talent, or much managerial complexity, press empires are well placed to avoid bureaucracy and, equally important, to promote creative independence and individuality.

Publishing managements fall quite naturally into a three-legged partnership, a *troika*, in which one boss sells the advertising, another edits the publication, and a third, the publisher or proprietor, directs policy. A Katherine Graham binds together the whole, in part by appointments, especially to the two other positions, but above all by determining the ethos, setting the style, defending the established values. Dictatorial, Hearst-like power can easily be applied from this position—but it isn't sustainable, as the Hearst heirs found.

Within a non-Hearst culture, editorial people are free to express their own talents (without which the commercial side has nothing worth selling) within an unusually flat structure: from editor to junior reporter (as from the *Post*'s Ben Bradlee to Woodward and Bernstein in the Watergate exposure) you may find no more than two intervening ranks, and more likely only one. In such a world of clearly defined, interlocking, nonhierarchical responsibilities, the top female executive seems quite natural, even to an editor who is male, as most editors are.

There's no longer a top female at the *Washington Post*,

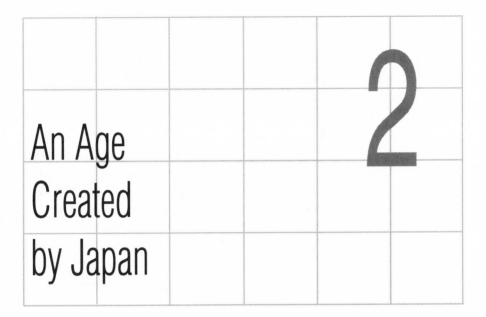

An Age
Created
by Japan

The record-breaking best-seller *In Search of Excellence*, which Thomas J. Peters wrote with Robert Waterman, was a recipe of comfort for the CEO (especially the American one, since all the excellent examples were American). It enshrined the existing order. It looked mostly inward (only one of the eight attributes of excellence, "continued contact with customers," a fairly mealy-mouthed formula, looked outward). It affirmed that you, the chief executive, could centrally command corporate success, making the company what you wanted in the way you wanted.

No wonder so many of the *Excellence* companies flopped. Today's necessity is to decentralize success, as recognized in Peters's own new creed, with its amazing change of emphasis from the earlier recipe. His latest inward-looking attributes number only four: flatness of organization, trust in people, high reward for high levels of achievement, and intensive training. All four are indispensable in a concept for effective management of men and women that doesn't look back to the 1980s but forward to the next century.

The four are the foundation stones for the outward attributes: market segmentation, innovation, responsiveness, relative perceived quality (RPQ), and relative perceived service (RPS). In this list, the issue is not, as before, merely contacting the customers, but satisfying them, by anticipating and serving their needs, and doing so better than the competition. Shifting the whole organization away from the interior to the exterior, from the center to the periphery, provides the best context for better management of people the whole way down: it gives the worker on the line, in the office, or in the retail outlet something near at hand to identify with, a center of achievement.

This identification of man and activity, the concept of the business as a harmonious social grouping, has marked one of the major divides between Western and Japanese practice, and it's very hard to believe that the concept bears no relation to Japanese success in W. Edwards Deming's "age created by Japan." Yet the notion that they order things better in Japan has taken a strangely long time to sink in. Robert Waterman's book *The Renewal Factor* is subtitled "Building and Maintaining Your Company's Competitive Edge." But I could find only four references to Japanese companies or individuals, even though Japan plainly has the most to teach about competitive edges and keeping same.

Peters has more references in his far longer book *Thriving on Chaos*, but a dozen and a half in a book of 523 pages verges toward the perfunctory. Yet the impact of Japanese methods, directly and indirectly, on management in the 1990s and beyond is likely to be at least as powerful, all over the industrialized world, as was that of the Americans on European management (and Japanese) in the 1950s and 1960s. There's still, however, controversy over the exact nature of Japanese methodology and the extent to which it can be emulated abroad. The debate is entirely phony—another excuse, conscious or subconscious, for ignoring the obvious.

It's true that cultural and mystical elements exist in Japanese management that can't be found easily, if at all, in the West. Some of these aspects, like the martial arts and philosophy of the samurai, have received too much attention in the West; others, like the influence of the delightful and practical philosophy of Zen, have received too little. There are certainly aspects of Japanese management that are foreign to most Western organizations, true, but not because the concepts are esoteric.

The theory that Japanese companies were managed in some very different, non-Western way wasn't much of a comfort anyway—because if the country's management were truly different, unrepeatable, and more effective, the contest would be over: game, set, and match to Japan. Increasingly, though, not only have Westerners been looking at Japanese management more objectively, but Japanese companies have begun operating production facilities in the West on a large and expanding scale. Numerous successful cases now exist to show that what works in Japan is truly operative in the West. The benefits of Japanese management are simply not unique to Japan, and it would be astounding if they were.

As Peter Drucker has observed, the three areas where the Japanese have established clear superiority over Western firms are quality control, production control, and effective mobilization of the human energies in the firm. All were learned initially from American teachers (respectively Deming, John Juran, and Drucker himself.) The world's most ravenous intellectual magpies, the Japanese snatch everything that glitters, test it for gold, and keep whatever passes the test.

American managers contemplating the Japanese in their midst are therefore looking at a mirror image of themselves, or rather would be, if they had taken any great notice of the Western gurus, absorbed their wisdom, and acted on it. That points to one enormously relevant and most easily imitated characteristic of Japanese management: it is thorough— "thorough" meaning not only painstaking, but through-and-through. That's where even some of the best Western competitors fall down.

miracle, given the impact on employment of the corporate upheavals dictated by the hierarchies. As the numbers of organization men have fallen, those of corporate entrepreneurs ("intrapreneurs" in the word made famous by Gifford Pinchot III) have probably increased. But this swing hasn't added up to any resurgence of the vibrant, large-scale capitalist enterprise from which most of today's great companies sprang.

Rather, the large Western organization has continued to suffer from defects that were identified by Xerox Corporation's Peter C. McColough three years before the Bennis book was published. How much of his 1963 indictment (Part I, Chapter 5) still holds true three decades later? Is McColough's cycle of "emergence, full flower of growth and prestige, and then later stagnation and death" truly inevitable? Must the "heavy hand of custom" stifle venture? Must habit and efficiency drive out flexibility and fresh ideas? And is there no escape from "the final stage of organizational senility," in which "there is a rule or precedent for everything"?

The endeavors of CEOs like IBM's John Akers to move the clock forward, when internal forces keep on turning it back, show that the problems identified by McColough persist. The halting and slow appearance of the organizational revolution forseen by Bennis points to a heavy inertia in the organization. That drag is deeply rooted in the need of human beings for order, position, permanence, authority, rules, power—all the classic features of bureaucracy. To remove deep roots requires radical action, and that demands radical men and women. As never before the manager must be a revolutionary, confident that anything and everything can be changed for the better along the whole of the spectrum of technology, distribution, and reputation.

Those who short-change any of the three do so at their peril. "Technology" needs to be redefined as the specification and quality of whatever product or service the company offers. Is the offering technically as good as or better than the best competition? Distribution describes the entire process of getting the product or service to the customers. Does it reach the widest possible market as effectively as that same competition—or more so?

Reputation is the sum total of technology, distribution, and promotion. Do all those you need to reach know about the company, and respond well to that knowledge, with a perception that equals or betters the best rival's? Getting the right answers to those three questions lays the foundations of the right business. The recurrent phrase "the best competition" only reflects the realities of modern markets, if your genuinely Unique Selling Proposition is in the same race with others. If it isn't, that's the ultimate in "competitive advantage."

It is most unlikely to be timeless. In Compaq's early life, uniqueness was achieved by concentrating only on portables. As portables have come down from the barely luggable to the briefcase and even pocket size, Compaq has been forced from sur-petition (in Edward de Bono's word) into competition—and itself lagged well behind Toshiba (still the leader) when the PC moved from lug to lap. The crucial trinity of technology, distribution, and reputation needs constant renewal: the continuous reexamination, reassessment, renovation, and, if necessary, replacement of parts of the recipe— for today even the best of companies can lose ground, which may be irrecoverable, by one false step.

Missteps are inevitable if a company gets locked into vested technical or marketing interests ("not invented here," "it will never work," etc.). Let the defense mechanisms win, and you will never exploit the most surefire means of success: achieving the "impossible." What enabled Compaq to transform its presence on the desktop—IBM's home ground—was redefining the possible. The "impossible" beating of IBM to the punch with the 386 chip consolidated the infant company's reputation in the crucial area of technology.

Once reputation has been built, it's a curious commodity. Beyond a certain point, it can't be raised much higher. If you have the high admiration and wide franchise of an IBM or a Motorola, major and sustained efforts are needed to maintain the customer following, let alone augment it.

The fact that adverse developments—like those devouring IBM's market share in PCs or Motorola's in microprocessors—took place in a sector involving the highest technology and fastest pace of change is irrelevant. The morals apply to any business.

As noted in Part I, Chapter 2, Compaq has asked the "failure mode effect analysis" question all along the line: what can go wrong, and what will be the effect if it does? That careful monitoring is one explanation of its successful run, up to the profit collapse of 1991. That last calamity carries a powerful moral, as the Motorola microprocessor story also tells: the best-managed companies can slip, and the impact of error now rushes upon managements so rapidly.

The buried and unburied mistakes of business haven't been spared in these pages, for they explain the loss of ground among great companies. Some of the major microeconomic blunders that still yawn as traps for firms of any country or size were identified by *Fortune* in April 1990:

1. Obsession with direct labor costs. In an age when these seldom amount to more than 15 percent of total expenses, that's looking at the wrong element of the business system.
2. Abandoning large businesses where low margins are causing problems. That can happen in any business as the product life cycle develops—but moving out simply hands present and future opportunity to somebody else, often for free.
3. Creating a mismatch between the product and the marketplace. That's the second fundamental going wrong—failing to achieve the right distribution.
4. Using resources to buy other companies (and your own shares) rather than to build established and new operations within the firm. Unless the buy strengthens technology, distribution, or reputation, what have you bought?

The magazine cited some awful examples to highlight these errors. (1) A firm making integrated circuits chose a new location for its low labor costs, even though labor was under 5 percent of the total. It was then crippled by the low literacy standards of the available work force. (2) Abandoning low-priced mass markets in early applications of solid-state electronics (the transistor radio) gave the Japanese competition unbeatable advantages in later uses like color TV. (3) Raytheon invented the microwave oven, but sold large appliances through traditional outlets. The Japanese sold smaller products through consumer electrical shops.

There's no point in listing (4) the cases of acquisition blunder, because they're endless. Decisions to purchase turnover and sales, instead of building them, often rest on faulty analysis of the same nature as wrongheaded decisions to chase labor costs or drop low-margin products. Making investments pass threshold rates of return or dropping out of markets (*à la* General Electric) because you can't claim first or second position isn't strategic thinking, but a tactical knee-jerk. The real issue is the long-run buildup of the company's technical and market strengths.

Motorola's Robert Galvin, one of America's outstanding business leaders (chairman of the executive committee, note, but not chief executive), has isolated the "biggest problem" in achieving this never-ending crescendo. He describes it as a question of leadership. "Total customer satisfaction" can't mean the corporation providing only the goods and services it wants to offer, though that has been the prevailing mode since time immemorial. Customers don't want only whatever the company is providing—they also want things that it is *not* providing, either by choice or by inadvertence.

Either way, the customer will satisfy those wants somewhere else, and the conventional wisdom will applaud. Businesses are advised to select and focus on what they can do well. Galvin argues, however, that in a generic business, the correct strategy is full-line competition; "you must offer everything they want." To follow that strategy, business leaders will have to change their orientation from the knee-jerk cutbacks that, for instance, caused the retreats from mass consumer electronic markets—see (2) above—and Raytheon's persistent reluctance, over many years, to commit corporate body and soul to microwaves (3).

It won't be easy to reverse the contraction and narrowing of the past decade or more. Galvin calls it "a giant challenge," which only a few companies, two or three handfuls, will meet. Half, in his view, will be U.S. and European; the others will all be Japanese. This merely recognizes the fact that Japan's leaders have instinctively followed a full-line policy, partly because of their inhibitions against abandoning businesses, partly because of the competitive reflex that drives them to exploit opportunities identified by others, partly because of their emphasis on building organically on what they have already created in technology and business systems.

Rafael Aguayo has good grounds for his view, looking at the differences of management between Japan and the United States, that "in effect, we have been conducting an experiment since 1950 between two very different styles," which "is as close as we could possibly come to conducting a controlled experiment on an international scale." He points out that W. Edwards Deming, the subject of his book, had predicted that "Japan would prosper while the United States and other nations following other methods wouldn't be able to compete. . . . The power of Deming's prediction about Japan, which he made in 1950 and which has since proved accurate, is that he made it before the results were known."

Those results can either be accepted fatalistically or used as the trigger for renewal, on the classic five-part cycle of crisis, review, restructure, focus, and development. To retain strength and momentum, the middle stages of the cycle (review, restructure, focus) should be applied while the development phase is still surging ahead—and on every one of the three dimensions, technology, distribution, and reputation. Companies that let this virtuous, overlapping cycle lapse won't need much "failure mode effect analysis" to discover the likely outcome: it's crisis, and these days crisis comes sooner rather than late.

That is the overriding strategic issue. But the greatest strategy in the world can be ruined by tactical blunders, and tactics in turn depend on basic principles. This book began by examining Operation Desert Storm for its relevance to